This b

The Unquiet Countryside

The Unquiet Countryside

Edited by
G. E. Mingay

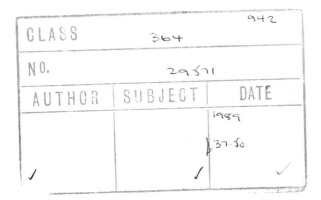

CLASS	942 364	
NO.	29571	
AUTHOR	SUBJECT	DATE
		1989
		£37.50
✓	✓	✓

Routledge

First published 1989
by Routledge
11 New Fetter Lane, London EC4P 4EE

© 1989 G. E. Mingay

Typeset in 10/12pt Times, Linotron 202, by
Input Typesetting Ltd, London
Printed in Great Britain
by T.J. Press (Padstow) Cornwall

British Library Cataloguing in Publication Data

The Unquiet Countryside
1. England. Rural regions. Crime 1600–1800
I. Mingay, G. E. (Gordon Edmund)
364′.942

ISBN 0–415–03426–4

Contents

The contributors

John E. Archer, Lecturer in History, Edge Hill College of Higher Education, Ormskirk

Pamela Horn, Lecturer in Economic and Social History, Oxford Polytechnic

David Jones, Senior Lecturer in History, University College, Swansea

G. E. Mingay, Emeritus Professor of Agrarian History, University of Kent at Canterbury

J. H. Porter, Senior Lecturer in Economic History, University of Exeter

John Stevenson, Reader in History, University of Sheffield

F. M. L. Thompson, Director, Institute of Historical Research, University of London

Editor's note

The essays which make up chapters 6–8 of this book first appeared in *The Victorian Countryside* (ed. G. E. Mingay, London: Routledge & Kegan Paul, 1981) and are reprinted here by kind permission of the authors. Chapters 1–5 were specially commissioned for this new volume.

Introduction

G. E. Mingay

Social relationships in the countryside of the past were very different in reality from those which might be conjured up by the pastoral pictures of poets, artists, and novelists. A human bond, fostered by long association, frequently existed between master and man, it is true; but very often it was weakened by mutual indifference, or never flourished because of the casual nature and brief endurance of the association. One might suppose however, that the affinity between the farmer and his farm servants – those hands hired by the year and accommodated and fed in the farmhouse or a nearby outhouse – was likely to be closer than any bond which grew up between the farmer and the day labourers; and much more so than the relationship with the specialist workers who were brought in only for occasional purposes, or the extra work-people taken on for haytime and harvest.

In the early part of the eighteenth century and before, farm servants made up between a third and a half of the hired labour force, and it seems probable that in the circumstances of the long-term nature of the hiring engagement, and the closeness of day-to-day contacts in and about the farmhouse, intimate ties of sympathy and understanding would have developed. The most recent study of this large class of work-people tells a different story, however. Farm servants were overwhelmingly young people, mainly aged between about 10 and 25, who were learning their farm skills; and, moreover, they frequently changed master, moving from one farm to another within a neighbourhood, often at every hiring.[1] Further, Hardy's picture of the hiring fair in *Far from the Madding Crowd* (which appeared in 1874, but referred to conditions earlier in the nineteenth century) suggests that the master's choice of a new man was in some degree haphazard and impersonal.[2] The farmer looked for a bailiff, a shepherd, ploughman or carter, whoever was required; he weighed up at a glance the age, physique, and character of the man; he asked briefly about his previous employment, and if matters were to his liking, sealed

1

the bargain with a shilling and a glass in a nearby tavern. The casual manner in which many farmers hired their men is borne out by documentary evidence for an earlier period – witness the Dorset farmer, James Warne, who recorded in his diary for 1758 how he engaged men who called at the house on the off-chance or who he met accidentally on the road when taking sheep to Weyhill Fair. And he parted with them just as readily, if they proved to be workshy or careless of his orders.[3]

Obviously, the dealings between master and man were likely to be more impersonal in a larger farm with a greater number of employees. Certain areas – the Norfolk sands, parts of Northumberland and Lincolnshire, and Salisbury Plain, for example – were noted for having extremely large farms, sometimes so extensive that one farm took up the whole parish. Moreover, the process of engrossing, the throwing together of small farms to form larger units, was said to be widespread in the eighteenth century. Contemporary assertions of this sort are upheld in some degree by the findings of research, which show that there was indeed a long-term tendency for farms to gradually grow in acreage, a trend that has been found both in areas of open-field farming as well as in those of old enclosure.[4] Furthermore, in prosperous periods, such as the war years between 1793 and 1815, successful farmers were able to expand their production and take over a number of nearby rented farms, employing their sons or bailiffs to manage the more distant enterprises. To the extent that these developments became important, the area was expanded over which one man or his representative controlled a work-force which, in the more extensive undertakings, might run into several scores of hands. Correspondingly, the situation became more common in which the master had little to do with the day-to-day running of the farm and was more or less remote from the lives and interests of the people he employed. Of course, many small farms remained, and even multiplied in number where market opportunities favoured the small man's specialities, such as dairying and market gardening, so that one should not exaggerate the changes that were occurring in the farming structure. The small farmer, employing no paid labourers at all, or very few, still dominated much the larger part of the countryside, and where one or two permanent labourers were employed, he had close personal relations with them.

But in so far as large-scale farming developed, so the large-scale farmer moved up the social ladder, and in means, appearance, and lifestyle moved further and further away from the situation of his work-people. By the middle of the nineteenth century, as described by a visiting French writer, he exhibited a calculating, business-like approach to his farming, standing in the middle of the yard 'in a black hat and black frock-coat', his expression cold and thoughtful, his orders given quietly and in few words.[5] Earlier than this farmers on the Coke estate in Norfolk, for example, were noted as living grandly with numerous house servants and a variety of carriages, while the large farmhouses on the Lincolnshire wolds could hardly be distinguished from the mansions of the gentry.

The social gap that developed between employer and man was widened further by a deterioration in the conditions of many work-people. The petty 'husbandman' of the eighteenth and earlier centuries, a semi-independent cultivator of a few acres of land, was increasingly replaced by the landless 'labourer', who rarely owned as much as the cottage he lived in, and was fortunate if able to keep a pig and grow his own vegetables in a garden or rented allotment. The gradual decline of the practice of 'living-in' reduced the numbers of farm servants over large parts of England (though not Wales), and their labour was increasingly replaced by that of day labourers. The security of the annual hiring (and the possibility of running some sheep along with the farmer's flock, enabling the servant to build up some stock towards taking his own farm) gave way to payment by the day. This form of hire, though it did not exclude long periods of employment on the same farm, was necessarily less secure for the labourer, and was likely to give rise to some unemployment as men were laid off in periods of bad weather and during slack times on the farm. Further, a tendency for many farmworkers, whether hired by the year or by the day, to move from farm to farm, and from district to district, inevitably weakened the personal connection with the employer.

By the early nineteenth century the bulk of English farmworkers had come to constitute a landless proletariat, almost entirely dependent on their wages, and relying for their livelihood and their home on masters who, increasingly, had come to regard them as 'hands', a labour force to be managed as economically as possible, rather than as workers known personally as individuals whose needs and problems might be treated sympathetically. The change was reinforced by the expansion of towns and the industrialization of many villages in the midlands and the north. Now, more than ever before, the countryman had the possibility of moving from farm to workshop, factory or warehouse; of becoming a town carter rather than a country one, or a groom or porter or postman or domestic servant; or of entering into the service of the police force, the army, or the railways. And, in growing numbers, he was attracted to try his fortune across the seas. The incentives and pressures to change home and occupation were intensified by the growth of the rural population, which despite the migration from the countryside, still exerted sufficient influence on the demand for employment to keep farm wages generally low; and in some areas of limited outward migration and absence of alternative occupations the wages were so low as to be miserably inadequate.

Indeed, if we were to point to only one factor as responsible, more than any other, for the decline of the farmworkers' living standards, then it would have to be the growth of population. (It should be noted that the decline in standards was perhaps more relative than absolute, that is to say, the farmworkers became more obviously worse off when compared to the improving standards of other groups in society.) The increase in the numbers, in the absence of sufficient migration to relieve its effects, together with the lack of alternative occupations as some old rural industries declined and disappeared, meant frequently enough that there was considerable unemployment among farmworkers; and where the labour demand was highly seasonal, the unemployment was heavily concentrated in the winter months. Moreover, increased numbers meant not only underemployment and constraint on wages, but also greater pressure on housing and more overcrowding when two- or three-room cottages had to shelter larger families. Diet and the care of the home suffered as the family income was stretched to feed more mouths and clothe more bodies; and the employment of farmworkers' wives on the land, and in country trades like lace-making and straw-plaiting, or in charring and taking in washing, while bringing more money into the home often left women exhausted and short of time, and so made home conditions worse. Poor diet contributed to poor health and loss of work through sickness; and inadequate nutrition, as was argued by nineteenth-century observers, resulted in the low level of work output noticeable in the areas of the lowest wages. In these areas, especially, there developed a vicious circle of inadequate wages – inadequate nutrition – inadequate productivity – and hence, inadequate wages. One reason for the poverty of many farmworkers in southern arable districts was that, apart from seasonal unemployment, they did not produce enough when working to encourage the farmers to reward them with a living wage.

A result of this situation was, necessarily, an increased dependence on poor relief, particularly in winter. Rural poor relief took many forms and varied greatly from parish to parish and from time to time, but commonly, as pressure of numbers forced up the poor rates, so the authorities tended to tighten up on whatever was given, with the Poor Law Amendment Act of 1834 marking the high point of middle-class alarm that the expenditure was excessive and that the methods of dispensing it contributed to idleness, shiftlessness, and widespread demoralization among the poor. The attempts to restrict relief, although general after 1834, were never fully effective, but the harsher, more grudging attitudes of the authorities towards claimants certainly played a part in the unrest of the period.

Dr Porter refers in chapter 1 to the significance for the level of crime of years of high food prices in the seventeenth and eighteenth centuries. And in a later period, too, when prices fell from the wartime peaks after 1815, the countryside was far from quiescent. Hunger, the result of low wages, larger families, unemployment, and meagre relief allowances, exerted a large influence on the major outbursts of 1816 in East Anglia, and of 1830 over eastern and southern England generally. 'Bread or blood' was not mere rhetoric, though indeed no lives, except those of some of the rioters, were lost in the outbreaks. 'He was starved', a magistrate was told by a rioter of 1816, who was subsequently transported for life, 'and he would be damned if he would not be fed'.[6] Rioters threatened, and in some cases actually assaulted, landowners, farmers, shopkeepers, Poor Law overseers, and also parsons – whose tithes were seen as a burden on the land which prevented farmers from paying better wages. They also broke machinery, devoting their major attention to the threshing machine, which reduced the winter employment obtained by the traditional and slow, if back-breaking, mode of beating out the corn with the flail. But, fundamentally, it was wages, food, and work that were at the bottom of the rioters' actions.

The large-scale riots of 1816 and 1830 were the most explicit attempts of hungry and desperate men to draw the notice of the governing class to their plight. But, stretching over a much longer period, other grievances were added to wages, employment, and poor relief, and to the widening that was evident of the economic and social distance between the employers and their work-people. These other sources of bitterness contributed to a variety of attacks on farmers' property, on machinery, hay-stacks, and barns, and on livestock, which if not entirely new, were certainly new in scale. Of course, there had always been many dep-redations on property in general, as Dr Porter's chapter shows. There were also food riots, as Dr Stevenson relates in chapter 2, though many offences of this kind originated with townspeople rather than country dwellers. In coastal areas (see pp. 15–16), smugglers were rife, working sometimes in gangs so large and well armed that they intimidated the authorities; and indeed the smugglers received active support from far-mers, who provided men, carts, and barns to assist in the traffic, while gentry and parsons passively accepted anonymous gifts of contraband and turned a blind eye to the nefarious business being conducted in their neighbourhood. In forested districts, too, where the arm of the law was notoriously feeble, gangs of robbers, highwaymen, forgers, and coiners could find refuge and indulge these occupations with little fear of disturb-ance. There were also in various parts of the country large villages, ones lacking resident squires or clergy, which were infamous for their sheltering of poachers and housebreakers, their drunken brawling, their opium taking, and their general dissipation and disrespect for the law. In total, large areas of the countryside, therefore, were very far from being havens of quiet peacefulness, and it is not surprising that respectable persons bold enough to venture out after dark preferred moonlit nights when they could better see their way and were less likely to run into footpads. And despite the increased employment of private gamekeepers and watchmen, the forces of law and order were often unequal to their task.

In the later eighteenth century, as the vogue for shooting and the consequent strict preservation of game developed, so a continual war came to be waged between magistrates and keepers on the one hand, and marauding poachers on the other. In the same period the enclosure by private Acts of Parliament of commons and waste lands for cultivation, greatly reduced the already limited areas over which cottagers could find pasture for a cow or gather fuel for their hearths; and, in addition, enclosures deprived local people of open woods and heaths where they could freely enjoy some sport in leisure hours: rambling, fishing, and snaring rabbits and birds. Accompanying the decline of common lands came a reduction in the number of customary holidays, and the suppression of pleasure fairs and of village wakes and 'revels' by magistrates concerned to check drunkenness and licentiousness. The countryside became more sober, more industrious, as Victorian morality and work ethic were brought to bear on the lives of working people. By contrast, the sports of the rich – hunting, shooting, riding, and racing – went on untouched, and the many contrasts in life and leisure were extended even to death, the elaborate family monuments in the graveyard genteelly distanced from the unmarked resting places of those too poor to leave any evidence that they had ever shared the same earth, air, and sky.[7]

To the universal nuisance of poaching were added the more localized but frightening activities of the arsonists, and the less frequent though intimidating depredations of the animal maimers, as described in chapters 4 and 5 by Dr Archer. Arson sometimes went beyond the burning of ricks and barns to the firing of the farmhouse itself, with the family in it; while maiming reached depths of depravity that must have horrified and nauseated those who saw the results. The 'counter-terror' of the poor sprang in some measure from the economic and social factors noted above, but it would be simplistic to suppose that these provided the whole explanation. Other influences emanated from the Revolution across the Channel – a convulsion dangerously inciting to the English poor, thought the reactionary observer, John Byng, who drew a bitter comparison between a duke's new kennels which he saw near St Neots and the 'miserable mud hovels' erected nearby for the poor:

> Here is little fuel to be bought, little to be pick'd up, but that is punished as theft, no land allot'd for potatoes, or ground for a cow: Agues devouring the children: Despondence overcoming the aged . . . It is from neglect, and despair that Democracy, that Anarchy, spring.[8]

Furthermore, through neglect and indifference, and through the counter-attraction of Nonconformity, the poor had become largely immune to any moral force exerted by the Church of England; while education, seen increasingly by the upper classes as the great civilizing influence that needed to be brought to bear on working people's ignorance, poverty, and tendency to riot, had not as yet made much headway in the countryside.

There are yet other considerations to be taken into account. The historical evidence indicates that rioting, poaching, and arson were predominantly the crimes of young men, and moreover, that they tended to be concentrated in particular areas. Much of the petty poaching done by individuals (as distinct from that carried out by gangs for profit) was the work of adventurous village lads to whom the existence of preserves and their keepers was a challenge, an irresistible attraction. Some of the arson, and no doubt some of the maiming, too, arose from personal rather than communal grievances, the paying off of old scores by workers unjustly discharged, men unsympathetically refused relief, or others who had felt the heavy hand of an overbearing overseer or stony-hearted magistrate. If farmers bore the brunt of the attacks (and many magistrates and overseers were farmers), they were, it might be remembered, very prominent among those bringing cases of felony to the courts. It is interesting that many of the incidents were ascribed to vagrants, itinerant gangs of workers passing through the neighbourhood, or other strangers, and not to local inhabitants, as if such offences could not be imagined as originating with people whose faces and histories were long familiar. There was evidently still some belief remaining in the survival of the close-knit, harmonious community, supposed to have existed in happier times.

The prominence of East Anglia and of Norfolk, in particular, in the history of rural crime is also interesting. And within that county, the names of certain villages crop up repeatedly. The riots of 1816 were concentrated in part of Norfolk, and it featured also in the much greater Swing riots of 1830, though not so markedly as some southern and western counties. Norfolk had its large arable farms, its wealthy landlords and well-to-do farmers, and its share of under-employment. Wages were low there, though not quite so low as in parts of some other counties of the southern half of England; and in Norfolk, as in the other low-wage districts, there were few occupations other than farming as the old local cloth industry fell into decay in the early nineteenth century. The county saw some parliamentary enclosure, but was by no means one of the most heavily affected, and indeed some commons remained there after enclosure. Perhaps the leading factors in Norfolk's lawlessness were the combination of low wages with remoteness from areas of expanding industries, and possibly the growth there of anti-clericalism and of strong bodies of Primitive Methodists, with their organization of working people, and their assertion of independence and self-reliance. The geography of rural crime raises intriguing questions which await further investigation.

There are indeed many questions that historians and historical geographers have not yet answered satisfactorily. But certainly the essays collected here go some considerable way towards providing solutions, and also open new insights into an aspect of English rural history that was little explored until quite recent years, and which generally is still little known beyond the readers of specialist studies. This book, it is hoped, will expand our understanding of the rural past, and will help to produce a more balanced comprehension of that romanticized mythical England of Squire Allworthy and Elizabeth Bennet, of Flatford Mill and Dingley Dell, of Barsetshire and John Jorrocks.

Notes

1 Kussmaul, 1981, 4, 51–9, 70, 79.
2 Thomas Hardy, 1874, *Far from the Madding Crowd*, chapter 6.
3 Dorset RO: D 406/1.
4 Mingay, 1961–2, 469, 481–2; Wordie, 1974.
5 Taine, 1957, 132.
6 Peacock, 1965, 64.
7 Porter, 1989, 880.
8 Andrews, 1954, 494–5, 506.

1

Crime in the countryside
1600–1800

J. H. Porter

The three most common types of crime in the two centuries after 1600 were property offences, assault, and offences relating to drink. This is an account of crime recorded principally before assize and quarter sessions, for we do not know the dark figure of unrecorded crime and informal justice in the village.

The evidence comes mainly from the southern counties of Essex, Hertfordshire, Surrey, and Sussex. At the turn of the century, 1601–2, 66 per cent of felonies in Essex comprised the stealing of livestock, chattels, or food, and a further 14 per cent the more serious offences of burglary, robbery, and forcible entry. [1] J. A. Sharpe's study of the Essex assize and quarter sessions for the period 1620–80 found larceny the most commonly indicted crime, with 2,653 cases being tried. The most common form of theft was that of sheep.[2] Another study of Essex quarter sessions, 1626–66, confirms the importance of theft,[3] while examination of the Hertfordshire and Sussex assizes by Professor Cockburn reveals for the former 1,018 indicted crimes, of which 828 were against property, and of those 600 were simple larceny.[4] Similarly Professor Beattie's recent investigation of assize and quarter sessions in Surrey and Sussex for 1660–1800 found 6,437 indictments in Surrey for crimes against property, of which 34.6 per cent were for simple grand larceny, 13.3 per cent for larceny, and 17 per cent for the more serious offences of robbery, burglary, and housebreaking. (Grand larceny applied to theft of goods valued at 1s. or more and was a capital offence; petty larceny to goods worth less than 1s., and was non-capital.) The figures for Surrey, however, are complicated by the county having both urban and rural parishes. Sussex, on the other hand, was pre-eminently rural. In that county there were 1,803 offences against property, of which 42.7 per cent were simple grand larceny and 25.2 per cent petty larceny. The three more serious property offences constituted 19 per cent of the total, and were thus similar to the Surrey finding, but the absolute number shows them to be of minor significance. The value of the goods stolen, even in simple grand larceny in the rural parishes, was low, the majority being below 5s. Of the goods stolen in the rural parishes of Surrey (petty and grand larceny) 26.5 per cent consisted of food, 21 per cent clothes, and 9.5 per cent household goods. In Sussex the respective figures were 29.2 per cent, 22.8 per cent, and 10.1 per cent. Sussex thieves had a particular liking for hens, geese, and ducks.[5]

In the south-western counties, studies of the Devon assize for 1700–9 show 76 per cent of indictments to be related to property offences, while in Cornwall during 1700–49 the figure was 80 per cent. In Norfolk and Suffolk between 1734 and 1737 85 per cent of offences were related to property.[6] Wiltshire indictments at quarter sessions between 1615 and 1624 show 45 per cent to be related to larceny.[7] The northern counties have been less intensively studied, but in South Lancashire quarter session prosecutions from the hundreds of Salford, Leyland, and West Derby in 1626–66 show 362 prosecutions for theft.[8] Before the Cheshire Court of Great Sessions, 1580–1709, 74 per cent of total indictments related to property offences.[9] Alan Macfarlane has concluded that in seventeenth-century Westmorland the various forms of theft of property were very common, while in the North Riding of Yorkshire between 1690 and 1750 a third of offences related to larceny, particularly of food and clothing.[10] Studies at parish and village level confirm this pattern. At Kelvedon in Essex, for instance, twenty-four property offences in the years 1600 to 1640 involved members of the parish, and they were the only frequent offences.[11]

The emphasis upon property offences can be illustrated further by the continual pilfering of wood and theft of sheep during the seventeenth and eighteenth centuries, to the extent that the latter was made a capital felony in 1741.[12] Roger Wells has recently stressed its widespread nature in Yorkshire, a county well stocked with sheep in the eighteenth century.[13] In Essex in 1620–80 19 per cent of larceny was sheep theft and, as in Yorkshire, clothiers were most suspect.[14] In Sussex and Surrey for a later period, 1660–1800, sheep stealing was dwarfed by all other thefts but there were still 43 and 73 indictments respectively (2.4 per cent and 1.1 per cent of the total).[15] Again, in the North Riding justices frequently dealt with sheep stealing.[16] The stealing of wood for fuel, especially in winter, was a constant irritation to landowners and farmers and was difficult to detect. Breaking hedges and stealing pales, trees, or faggot wood were common throughout the countryside. In Wiltshire in 1784, for example, ten men stole fencing round the Earl of Portsmouth's park, and in Hampshire it was a 'daily practice to tear hedges'.[17]

Before turning to physical assault or 'interpersonal violence' we should notice the kinds of verbal abuse which could suck a small community into

a vortex of enmity. Cases of defamation of character, scolding, and barratry (the spreading of false rumours) might come before the church courts
or the justices' sessions. Frequently the dispute arose from a long-standing
quarrel, an impetuous argument, or other disruptive behaviour. Thus
Alice Crathorne of Seasalter in Kent was charged in 1616 with being 'a
common swearer and brawling scold . . . drunk exceedingly'. Between
1615 and 1624 twelve cases of barratry and scolding came before the
Wiltshire justices, including one concerning Katherine Farmer of Compton
Bassett, who in 1620 had composed a libelous song.[18] In 1651 Edward
Constable of Aveley in Essex was indicted for barratry and was twice
bound over to keep the peace with his wife. They were obviously a
troublesome couple for the wife had also been indicted for barratry in
1639.[19] The damage to reputation and social relations can be illustrated
by citing the situation at Long Cliffe in Yorkshire in 1696, where gossip
about a woman's possible pregnancy led another to denounce scandal-
mongers, for 'they might as well take her life as take her good name from
her'. Defamation suits most affected the middling sort and were most
common in the first half of the seventeenth century.[20] Upsetting to village
life as scolding was, it is difficult to tell how widely it occurred. Present-
ments before the Deaneries of Doncaster in 1610 and 1633, Frodsham in
1630 and 1633, Sudbury in 1633, and also Crewkerne and Dunster show
it to be rare in those samples.[21]

Assault was more frequently tried, at least up to the Restoration, before
the manorial courts rather than the higher courts of quarter sessions and
assize. For example, in the Lancashire manor of Prescott in 1615–60, 1,252
inhabitants of the manor were presented for assault at the leet court,
compared with only 23 who came before the quarter sessions.[22]
An extreme case was a certain Evan Pike. In 1623 he was charged
with twenty-three assaults, twice with drunkenness, and once with breaking the courthouse windows. Yet he was not sent before the justices.
Similarly, at Upholland Ralph Whalley was charged over the years
1603–23 with twenty-five assaults, as also was Nicholas Taylor. Only
once was Taylor brought before the justices, and that was for fighting a
constable.[23]

In the Essex village of Terling in the seventeenth century, 43 inhabitants
were involved in assault cases, and at Essex quarter sessions held between
1626 and 1666 255 assault cases were prosecuted, the second most important category of offences after those concerning property.[24] Over the period
1620–80 in Essex 17 per cent of indictments at quarter sessions concerned
assaults.[25] Hertfordshire and Sussex in 1603–25 had respectively 31 and
42 cases of assault, while in Wiltshire in 1615–24 the 118 indictments made
assault the second most important crime.[26] The north may have seen more
assault than the better-ordered south, for in the North Riding in 1690–1750
assault took up, after larceny, almost all the court's record of criminal

offences.[27] And in the three Lancashire hundreds of Salford, Leyland, and West Derby in 1626–66, 800 cases of assault came before the quarter sessions, three times the figure for Essex.[28]

Central to village life was the alehouse. It was central, too, to those in authority who saw drink as a force undermining society and the economy, and weakening the individual both financially and morally. According to the Act of 1604 alehouses were 'not meant for entertainment and harbouring of lewd and idle people to spend and consume their money in a lewd and drunken manner', and the seventeenth century was to see frequent purges of both licensed and unlicensed houses. In Essex in the 1630s there was one alehouse for every 125 inhabitants.[29] In 1638 there were 2,000 licensed and 500 unlicensed alehouses in the West Riding, while in south Lancashire in 1647 30 townships had 83 licensed and 143 unlicensed alehouses. That much drinking took place on Sundays further dismayed the respectable; in 1613 it was reported in a Worcester parish that the twenty-six alehouse keepers 'neither frequent church themselves nor warn their guests to do so in time of divine service'.[30] Furthermore, the tendency for alehouses to spread into marginal areas of woods, hills, and heathlands made them the more suspect to authority, and especially as their keepers were frequently poor or were newcomers to the village. By 1670, however, brewster sessions had been adopted in most counties, and by 1700 the rural alehouse was under control.[31]

In Essex prosecutions of unlicensed alehouses were concentrated in the years 1645–54 and especially in years of bad harvests; between 1620–80 there were 1,682 prosecutions of unlicensed alehouses in the county.[32] In south Lancashire there was a sudden drive against alehouses in 1646–8: out of a total of 1,290 unlicensed alehouse offences brought between 1626–66, 45 per cent fell in those years.[33] In Cheshire after 1645 the grand jury concerned itself with keeping down the number of alehouses and drew attention to villages where there were too many of them,[34] East Riding justices in 1651 were also much concerned with drunkenness, and their North Riding colleagues held purges in 1616 and 1619, and indeed continued to do so, as for example in 1718 when 190 unlicensed houses were presented.[35]

The list of petty offences is evidence of the centrality of the alehouse to village life from Cornwall to the northern borders. In 1630 the justices at Launceston informed 'the mayor and corporation of Tregoney . . . that thirty-six alehouses in the town is too many'. They were still complaining of excess alehouses in the county in 1674.[36] Typical of prosecutions of customers was one of 1600, when the accused was a Thomas Carr of Billericay, Essex, who lived idly, 'going from alehouse to alehouse spending his time'.[37] At Kelvedon in Essex John Ayley was frequently prosecuted for disturbing the sabbath and for encouraging drinking and swearing.[38] Before the Somerset assizes in 1630 Richard Gash, alehouse keeper, was described as 'a lewd fellow and has kept much ill rule'.[39] There, too, another alehouse keeper, John Clarke of Dunyatte, was sent to the house of correction for brewing unlicensed beer and allowing 'tippling' or continual drinking.[40] In 1611 the Cheshire grand jury proceeded against William Thompson and John Dennper of Newton, 'who kept tippling houses and do entice people at unreasonable times'.[41] Finally, when the respectable of Waltham Cross presented John Bowden, it was complained that he persistently harboured vagrants in his disorderly alehouse 'to the great disquiet of his neighbours'.[42]

The vagrant was often seen as a threat to order, although recent research stresses that the typical vagrant was a member of the displaced poor rather than a picturesque rogue. However, the pattern of vagrant movement, from west to east and from highland to lowland regions, meant continual suspicion of such strangers, and whip and workhouse were the customary punishments for vagrancy in the seventeenth century.[43] Vagrants travelled in ones and twos, often via local alehouses, with such individuals as Edward Miller in Essex, described in 1655 as 'a wandering fellow who sometimes begged and sometimes wrought'.[44] Vagrants, however, were prone to opportunistic theft from isolated dwellings and the taking of goods left unattended. Thus in 1620 a Wiltshire weaver, Anthony Hooper, found himself unemployed and took to travelling about to subsist on harvest work. When that ceased he stole some clothes from a hedge while on the way home and was indicted and whipped.[45] Villages feared that vagrants would become squatters and a burden on the parish, and so we find in the East Riding in 1647 the parishioners of Settrington petitioning the justices for their removal.[46]

All this presents a picture of opportunistic rather than organized crime. There are, however, some examples of itinerant gangs operating in rural Surrey in the eighteenth century, and also in the Midlands,[47] and there were the occasional professional sheep stealers or horse thieves. Gangs, however, as at Bocking in Essex in 1627, or at the Smorthwaites in Westmorland, were exceptional.[48] The only organized crime that was common in rural areas was smuggling.

Regional and temporal differences

It is generally assumed that the north was more unruly than the south, and that upland and forested areas, in particular, were more likely to harbour criminals. According to Alan Macfarlane, the barbarism of the north has been much exaggerated, for in Westmorland he could find few cases of violence over the years 1650–99.[49] Nevertheless, people of Pennine Lancashire were described as 'ignorant', and those of upland Northumberland 'rude', and a study of the northern circuit assize for the late seventeenth century suggests a higher level of assault than in the south. Even in Northumberland and Cumberland, however, property offences remained the dominant crime.[50] During 1626–66 assault was more common in south Lancashire than in well-governed Essex.[51] Cloth workers were particularly fractious – as in Essex clothing districts in 1620–80, for example, or in eighteenth-century West Riding.[52] Proximity to London was also likely to promote property crime in proportion to other offences. Offences against property in Sussex in 1603–25 made up 25 per cent of the total of indicted crimes, while in Hertfordshire they formed 81 per cent.[53]

The assessing of trends in reported crime is notoriously hazardous, the finding of causes even more so. If the ratio of prosecuted crime to all crime was low, even small changes in the behaviour of prosecutors would have far greater effects on the movement of indictments than would quite large changes in the behaviour of offenders.[54] Bearing this in mind, what long term trends are revealed for crime in the countryside? Prosecution of all felonies, and especially property offences, showed a marked drop between the early seventeenth and early eighteenth centuries. Court records for Essex, Sussex, and Hertfordshire for 1559–1625, Cheshire for 1580–1709, Essex for 1620–80, Sussex and Surrey 1660–1800, Devon 1700–9, Cornwall 1700–49, and Norfolk and Suffolk 1734–7, all confirm this. The rising trend in crime in Elizabethan times seems to have continued until the end of the 1620s. In Essex property offences were at least three times more common in the years 1625–34 than they were in the 1660s.[55] In Cheshire indictments for felony rose steadily in 1580–1629, reaching a peak in the 1620s, then declining during the 1640s and remaining static for the rest of the seventeenth century. In Cheshire the Court of Great Sessions tried only one felon in the August of 1760. In the 1660s that same court sent 166 to the gallows. Records for mid-eighteenth-century Cheshire suggests that the low levels of crime and executions continued. In both Essex and Devon prosecutions during the first decade of the eighteenth century formed only a small portion of those which came before the courts in 1597–1631.[56]

In rural Sussex and rural Surrey the number of bills brought to the grand jury fell steadily for more than a hundred years after the Restoration until about 1770, when the decline was reversed. In the last two decades of the eighteenth century there was a rise in property offences in both of these rural areas and a new pattern of much sharper annual fluctuations appeared. Over the period 1660–1800 as a whole there was a change of criminal behaviour in the apparent decline of violent forms of property crime, and further, attitudes towards violence and the character of violence itself seem to have changed in some significant ways in the later eighteenth century.[57]

How may the fluctuation in prosecutions be explained? Two causes seem paramount, food prices and war. In Essex over the sixty years between 1620 and 1680 the three periods of the sharpest rise in wheat prices were all marked by corresponding rises in property offences, especially in 1629–31, when a textile depression coincided with bad harvests.[58] Most of the rural working population were subject to sharp variations in their standard of life, and in times of distress prosecutions rose in the rural parishes of Surrey and Sussex, for example in 1740–2, when work was often in short supply. If high prices coincided with return to peace then the problem was compounded because the labour market was glutted with discharged and disreputable soldiers, men brutalized by war. The *Salisbury Journal* reported in 1783 that 'a great number of disbanded militia men, who are too idle to return to their farming business, are robbing all parts of the country'; conversely, in wartime such men were taken out of the country and out of the labour market.[59] The significance of food prices and the availability of work has been studied for Staffordshire over the period 1742–1802 by Douglas Hay, who claims that if dearth and peace coincided the effect on property crime figures was greater than if either occurred singly.[60] Food prices may not only explain fluctuations but also contribute to the long-term trend. Over the century following the Restoration the trend in prices was broadly in favour of the consumer; after 1760 this ceased to be so and, moreover, the labourer was increasingly wage-dependent.[61] At village level, at Terling in Essex, for example, the long-term changes in crime confirm the patterns discovered by Dr Sharpe and Professor Beattie.[62]

Smuggling and wrecking

There are two kinds of crime in the countryside which do not follow these trends and moreover, differed in that they also enjoyed a popular legitimacy: smuggling and wrecking. The heyday of smuggling was from the late seventeenth century and on throughout the eighteenth century as duties on imports were increased, a policy arising from the ideology of mercantilism and the necessity to finance the wars against France. Smuggling touched all sections of society and may have been widely accepted but it was accompanied by much intimidation, and in the south-east in particular, by considerable brutality.

In the north the Isle of Man was the centre for smugglers supplying Wales, north-west England, Cumberland, and south-west Scotland. From Ireland tea and spirits were landed on the Welsh coast and Anglesey, but the Isle of Man ceased to be a base after its purchase by the government from the Duke of Atholl in 1765.[63]

From Plymouth to Land's End south-western smugglers took their contraband from Guernsey – tea, brandy, rum, tobacco, cloth, and wine. A survey of 1764 showed Guernsey to be supplying Hampshire and Dorset as well, with the ultimate destination the London market.[64] The south-western 'freetraders' were less violent than the organized gangs of Kent and Sussex, but brute force was not uncommon among them. In 1735, for example, the excise men were attacked when a quantity of rum was found in a barn near Fowey in Cornwall; and on another occasion, in 1768, the excise officer at Porthleven was murdered.[65] In neighbouring Devon in 1787 two officers were murdered by smugglers on the road between Honiton and Beer,[66] and in 1766 a William Hunt was 'most barbarously wounded' by smugglers from Beer.[67] Off the north Devon coast Lundy was a smugglers' centre, particularly after 1748 when it was under the ownership of a Bideford merchant, Thomas Benson.[68]

The coasts of the Isle of Wight, Dorset, and Hampshire were favourite landing points for the smuggling trade, and villages on the routes to London became centres for the gangs, especially in wooded and isolated areas. Inland from Portsmouth, the village of Cheriton in the Itchen valley was well placed for the smugglers, as were Wooten in the New Forest, and also Burley and Fordingbridge.[69] The gangs were often numerous and dangerous. On Chesil beach in 1717 Dorset smugglers assembled 30 men 'in disguises and armed with clubs', and two years later there was a twelve-hour battle inland from Lulworth during which much of the contraband was carried off by 'the country people'. In Sherborne smugglers even had themselves elected as constables to obstruct the revenue officers. Other battles took place at Mudeford in 1784 and at Hook Wood in Cranborne Chase in 1786. Wiltshire smugglers traded through Dorset, and in 1770 a riding officer was viciously attacked by a gang of smugglers, sixty strong, coming from Downton.[70]

It was, however, the organized and violent gangs of Kent and Sussex who achieved most notoriety, with a guerilla war constantly raging between them and local authority as embodied in the Duke of Richmond. Sussex smugglers extended their trade to Hampshire, and in Kent the village of Hawkhurst and its gang became notorious for the battle at nearby Goudhurst, where in 1747 the Hawkhurst gang attempted to burn down the town. This gang was infamous, too, for their brutal torture and murder of the tide-waiter Galley, and of an informer, Chater, from Fordingbridge. Less extreme but still violent measures might be applied against other opponents. Farmer Alexander Carr of Beddington in Sussex, suspected in 1749 of being an informer, had his windows broken, was sent a threatening letter, and found his barns opened and cattle destroyed. In a two-year campaign the Duke of Richmond saw thirty-five smugglers hanged, while a further ten only escaped the gallows by dying in gaol.[71]

In contrast to smuggling, wrecking was more localized. Though not confined to their boundaries, wrecking was a speciality of the Cornish and the Welsh, and in general was a function of the increasing trade of the eighteenth century. Wreckers did not, in fact, lure ships on to rocks but appropriated the cargoes once they had become stranded. Again there was a conflict between perceived customary right and the legal rights of private property. The miners, farmers, and labourers of Cornwall were the most adept at the practice, and we have an example from as early as 1650, the *Aleppo Merchant*, looted in the neighbourhood of Padstow. In 1738 even the presence of troops could not protect a Hamburg vessel from 'the country people', and in 1764 miners of Perranazabuloe even carried away the clothes off the backs of the crew of the French vessel *Marrianne*.[72]

Wrecking also occurred on the Welsh coast, and in 1782, for example, three people were shot in a confrontation at Bridgend; off Anglesey in 1774 the captain of a vessel and his wife, the sole survivors, were mercilessly stripped and plundered. Plundering was also known elsewhere – off the Wirral, for instance, and on the Kent coast. A ship grounded on Goodwin Sands in 1774 had almost been refloated when 200 men arrived on the scene from Deal, prevented the ship's escape and plundered it.[73]

Typical law breakers and their motives

The early seventeenth century saw not only the ordinary villagers but the parochial elite involved in offences, particularly those of barratry and assault. Northern depositions suggest that the gentry were as willing participants in brawls as their social inferiors. Similar evidence in Essex comes from Earls Colne and Terling, and also at Kelvedon, where a clothier, Osias Johnson, was a frequent offender over the years 1609–21, being involved in fighting in 1614 and assaulting a constable in 1619, for example. Nevertheless, evidence from Essex, Surrey, and Sussex suggests that as the century progressed there was a growing tendency for criminal and disorderly behaviour to be viewed as synonymous with the poor. As Peter Clark puts it, few honest poor could have survived.[74]

Professor Beattie emerges from his study of court records in Surrey and Sussex with the conviction that most men, given the opportunity to work, would do so; and that when employment was available and prices were moderate, property crime was likely to be at a low level. When the reverse was true, as in 1629–31 or 1741, then it was necessary to survive by stealing. In particular, disbanded men could not find work, nor often could vagrants. In very hard times grand juries were liable to recognize this and consequently increased the numbers of discharges and downcharging.[75] Thefts of foodstuffs and clothing suggest necessity, as does sheep stealing, and many before the courts claimed destitution. Thus, Agnes Slade of Melksham stole a sheep in the 1622–3 dearth 'for want, and she had not food to relieve her and her child they being famished'.[76] Similarly, Whitby labourers in 1786 stole sheep, 'not having any bread or meat'.[77]

Then there were those more disorderly persons who were the bane of village life: persistent trouble makers, petty thieves, and drunkards. Such were two men from South Ickendon in Essex, who in 1664 were 'generally known to be constant night-walkers, deer stealers, sheep stealers . . .

17

cheat, idle and lazy fellows'. So, too, was George Gossage of Myddle in Shropshire, who crowned a career of thief, drunkard, counterfeiter, and poisoner by poisoning himself.[78]

Those in the food trades, the butchers and alehouse keepers, could make a pecuniary gain from stolen sheep or fowls. The latter, too, were suspected of encouraging drunkenness to their profit. However, many crimes relating to drink were crimes without victims, and relate more to the diverging mores of the village respectability and the poor rather than an inherent criminality of the latter.[79] In assault also it is difficult to distinguish motives when personal and family disputes, petty jealousy, and the natural tensions of a face-to-face community were the constant features of a constrained village life; and it was this complexity that made resort to binding over so common.

Punishment and the law

In the eighteenth century a wider range of punishment became available and the proportion of criminals subjected to judicial violence diminished. At the apex of retribution stood the gallows: in Essex there were 50 hangings in the years 1601–2; and between 1620 and 1680 at least 436 persons were hanged at assizes in the county, certainly an underestimate.[80] Devon saw 74 death sentences passed between 1598 and 1639, while in the 1620s Cheshire Great Sessions sent 166 to the gallows. Other public penalties included branding, the stocks or pillory, and whipping. While Dr Sharpe has found that use of the stocks and pillory was rare in Essex, Lancashire justices commonly whipped both men and women stripped naked to the waist, and put them in the stocks. And at Pocklington in the East Riding of Yorkshire the justices ordered a sheep stealer of 1648 to be whipped there while the market was in progress 'upon his naked shoulders till the blood comes'.[81] In most counties in the seventeenth century there were hangings twice a year following the assizes, while the quarter sessions produced a large number of convicted offenders to be whipped in public or flogged through the streets on market day. The vagrant was taken to a house of correction (established in 1610), where he would be whipped several times and set to labour.

In common law a crucial distinction was made between petty and grand larceny, the latter being punishable by death, though as for other less serious offences, it was subject to 'benefit of clergy', meaning that exemption from first conviction would be enjoyed by all who could read. This distinction disappeared in 1706, when the right to benefit of clergy was extended to all convicted offenders of minor offences, who could now be sent to the house of correction. Another major change was the Transportation Act of 1718, which allowed both grand and petty larcenists to be sent to the colonies. The result, therefore was that wider alternatives to hanging and public whipping became available in the first two decades of the eighteenth century, and the exhibition of public violence in the countryside was thus diminished.[82] Evidence from the south-eastern counties, and from Cheshire and Devon, shows a trend towards fewer hangings.[83] So while there was an increase in capital statutes over the whole period 1688–1820, [84] the proportion of convicted persons hanged declined in the eighteenth century, and especially after 1760 when imprisonment became well established as a possible sanction for felony. Burning in the hand of clergy was abolished in 1779, and a wider range of fines imposed. In particular, a growing antipathy to public violence showed itself in the last two decades of the eighteenth century. Hanging, nevertheless, remained at the core of the system, and while the proportion punished in this way diminished, the actual number hanged each year did not necessarily fall. For example, more men were hanged in Surrey in the 1790s than in the 1690s.[85]

Effectiveness of enforcement

The enforcement of the law was subject to discretion at many levels of the decision-making process, which recent research suggests resulted in increased effectiveness and also confirmed its general acceptability. The prosecutors, witnesses, neighbours, and parish officials, the magistrates as community officers or as summary courts, grand and petty juries, trial judges and quarter sessions bench, even the Secretary of State and the Crown, could all be involved in law enforcement. Prosecutors were not limited to a narrow band of gentry. Over one-third of those bringing felony cases in Essex before the quarter sessions in 1760–1800 were farmers or yeomen, while only 5.5 per cent were gentry prosecutions. In proportion to their share of the population the farmers were the most active group. More than one-fifth of prosecutions for felony and assault were by labourers or husbandmen, so as a class they did not meet the law only as criminals, but like other classes were concerned to protect both their person and their household goods. This is not to say there was consensus about the law, for different groups had different ideas and usages, but there was a general trust in its broad principles.[86] Discretion during the legal process, then, was not confined to the rulers of England, as has been suggested.[87]

In part, the efficient administration of justice depended on a sufficiency of resident justices, and the seventeenth century saw an improvement in county administration, particularly after the Book of Orders of 1630–1 set assize judges to supervise justice more closely. Remote areas, such as Cleveland, for instance, might be lacking in resident justices, although by the end of the eighteenth century the growth in the number of clerical magistrates had generally eased this difficulty. Villagers, like the state

itself, disliked disruption and the frequency of binding-over orders indicates their acceptance of at least that part of the law.[88]

Local order depended upon village officers successfully mediating in a
trouble before it went out of village hands; their object was to avoid
disruptive conflict. While some justices might complain of idle or dissolute
constables, the returns of 1642 showed those of Somerset and Dorset to
be highly literate and effective, and it seems probable that the difficulties
of filling the office have been exaggerated. Further, their flexibility was
not in fact inefficiency but a desire to avoid remote sanctions until they
were needed as a last resort.[89]

The law took into account two factors, the existing level of crime and
the character of the defendant. The discretion in the system at each stage
– up to three dozen men might be involved in the decision process before
the ultimate penalty of the gallows was reached – allowed the character
of the prisoner and the wider social needs to be served by verdict and
penalty. Further, the moral underpinnings of the law constrained as well
as inspired the men whose decision determined punishment. Ultimately
the operation of the law, as it applied to common crime in the countryside,
depended upon its acceptance by a broad spectrum of rural society.[90]
There might be a growing distance between respectable and vulgar values
but by 1800 uncivilized behaviour was not in itself defined as criminal.

Notes

1 Emmison, 1970, 318.
2 Sharpe, 1983, 92–3.
3 Wrightson, 1980, 303–5.
4 Cockburn, 1977, 55.
5 Beattie, 1986, 54–5.
6 Sharpe, 1983, 54–5.
7 Ingram, 1977, 112.
8 Wrightson, 1980, 300–5.
9 Sharpe, 1983, 54–5.
10 Macfarlane, 1981, 186; Cockburn, 1965, 491.
11 Sharpe, 1977, 100.
12 Rule, 1982, 106–15.
13 Wells, 1984, 127–45.
14 Sharpe, 1983, 92–3.
15 Beattie, 1986, 158–9.
16 Cockburn, 1965, 491.
17 Bushaway, 1982, 207–33; Beattie, 1974, 79.
18 Bridenbaugh, 1968, 359; Ingram, 1977, 112, 121.
19 Sharpe, 1983, 158.
20 Sharpe, 1980a, 3–23.
21 Marchant, 1969, 218.
22 Sharpe, 1984, 26.
23 Walter J. King, 1980, 311–12.
24 Wrightson and Levine, 1979, 120; Wrightson, 1980, 300–1.

25 Sharpe, 1983, 115, 183.
26 Cockburn, 1977, 55; Ingram, 1977, 112.
27 Cockburn, 1965, 491.
28 Wrightson, 1980, 300–1.
29 Sharpe, 1983, 50–5.
30 Wrightson, 1981, 1–27.
31 Clark, 1978, 47–72.
32 Sharpe, 1983, 182–97.
33 Wrightson, 1980, 301.
34 Morrill, 1976, 36.
35 Forster, 1975, 121; Forster, 1973, 36; Cockburn, 1965, 490.
36 Cockburn, 1976, 16, 263.
37 Emmison, 1970, 212.
38 Sharpe, 1977, 102–3.
39 Cockburn, 1976, 10.
40 Barnes, 1959, 18.
41 Curtis, 1977, 139.
42 Wrightson, 1980, 30.
43 Beier, 1974, 1–29; Slack, 1974, 360–79.
44 Sharpe, 1983, 170.
45 Ingram, 1977, 133.
46 Forster, 1973, 47–8.
47 Beattie, 1986, 252–4; Sharpe, 1984, 106–7.
48 Sharpe, 1983, 110–13; Wells, 1984, 137–9; Macfarlane, 1981, *passim*.
49 Macfarlane, 1981, 9, 186.
50 Sharpe, 1984, 57.
51 Wrightson, 1980, 300–3.
52 Sharpe, 1983, 208.
53 Cockburn, 1977, 53.
54 Innes and Styles, 1986, 390–5.
55 Cockburn, 1977, 53; Sharpe, 1983, 182–209.
56 Sharpe, 1983, 214–17.
57 Beattie, 1974, 47–95; Beattie, 1986, 11, 107–14, 138–9, 202–5.
58 Sharpe, 1983, 182–209.
59 Beattie, 1986, 202–36.
60 Hay, 1982, 117–60.
61 Beattie, 1986, 202–36; Cockburn, 1965, 491.
62 Wrightson and Levine, 1979, 114–15.
63 Carson, 1972, 65–103; Jamieson, 1986, 195–219.
64 Jamieson, 1986, 195–219; Jackson, 1986, 5–21.
65 Jenkin, 1932, 4–27.
66 Coxe, 1984, 3–34.
67 Carson, 1972, 77; Rattenbury, 1837, 28–9.
68 Thomas, 1959, 12–15, 48–51.
69 Morley, 1983, 40–3, 71–7, 97, 127.
70 Guttridge, 1987, 15, 22, 44–5.
71 Winslow, 1975, 119–65.
72 Clive Carter, 1970, 140–1; Jenkin, 1932, 91; Rule, 1975, 167–88.
73 Rule, 1975, 168–70, 179; Carson, 1972, 108–17; Muskett, 1986, 46–72.
74 Sharpe, 1983, 119, 162–75; Cockburn, 1977, 97; Ingram, 1977, 116; Beattie, 1975, 107.
75 Sharpe, 1983, 119–220; Beattie, 1986, 171, 186, 405.

76 Ingram, 1977, 133.
77 Wells, 1984, 133.
78 Sharpe, 1983, 166–7; Hey, 1974, 149.
79 Sharpe, 1980b, 97–118.
80 Emmison, 1970, 319; Sharpe, 1983, 142–51.
81 Sharpe, 1984, 70–1; Marchant, 1969, 224.
82 Beattie, 1986, 74, 88–9, 143, 182, 608–21.
83 Sharpe, 1984, *passim*.
84 Hay *et al.*, 1975, 17–63.
85 Beattie, 1986, 55–67, 88–9, 138–9, 576–88.
86 P. J. R. King, 1984, 25–58.
87 Hay *et al.*, 1975, 48.
88 Sharpe, 1984, 143–67, 214–17; Beattie, 1986, 60–3.
89 Wrightson, 1980, 22–30; Sharpe, 1980b, 97–119; Sharpe, 1984, 117–22; Beattie, 1986, 268–90.
90 Beattie, 1986, 323–5; Herrup, 1985, 102–23; Macfarlane, 1981, 197.

2

Bread or blood

John Stevenson

In eighteenth-century England the most characteristic form of popular protest was riot, and riots occurred on a wide range of issues. However, the most persistent and widespread were those associated with food, and it has been estimated that something in the order of two out of every three disturbances were of this type.[1] Food riots covered a wide but well-defined range of activities, such as stopping the movement of grain, forcible seizure and resale of food, often at 'fair' or traditional prices, the destruction of mills and warehouses, the spoiling of foodstuffs, and various kinds of tumultuous assembly to force dealers or local authorities to reduce prices. In its classic form the food riot could be found in many parts of western Europe between the seventeenth and the twentieth centuries. It was usually characterized by a high degree of discipline amongst the rioters, the use of ritual elements, and concentration upon those specifically concerned with the trade in foodstuffs and the setting of prices.[2]

There is evidence of food rioting as early as the 1520s and a series of disturbances have been found in the sixteenth and seventeenth centuries. usually associated with years of harvest failure and high prices, such as the 1520s, 1590s, and 1620s. It has been suggested that there were at least forty incidents of food rioting between 1585 and 1660 which can be verified from the records of central government. Although this total is regarded as an underestimate, the conclusion is that the years of dearth in early modern England 'were not marked by widespread rioting'.[3] Food rioting certainly took place in early modern England, but it never reached the scale of later years. Available research suggests that food riots only became common towards the latter part of the seventeenth century, accompanying periods of high prices in the mid–1670s, mid–1690s, and 1708–9. But it was during the eighteenth century that food riots became most pronounced, occurring with increasing frequency as the century wore on and only dying out in the first half of the nineteenth century. A number of nation-wide waves of food rioting have been identified after 1714 and related to periods of harvest failure or trade depression, such as those of 1727–9, 1739–40, 1756–7, 1766–8, 1772–3, and 1783. The years of the French Revolution and the Napoleonic Wars saw food rioting reach new heights with major periods of disturbance in 1795–6, 1800–1, 1810–13, 1816–18. Thereafter, food riots were confined to the remoter parts of the British Isles. By the mid-nineteenth century, the tradition of popular food riots in Britain was virtually dead, though it survived in other parts of Europe until the twentieth century.[4]

The pre-conditions for the frequent appearance of food rioting in this period was the dependence of the majority of the population upon a limited range of staple foods, of which the most important was bread. The budgets of this period make it clear that bread formed the most important part of the diet of ordinary people. Although the amount of bread consumed varied between different parts of the country and gradations of income and status, the great bulk of the population consumed at least a pound of bread a day by the middle of the eighteenth century. Sir Frederick Eden at the end of the eighteenth century found from a wide variety of sources, including the dietaries of workhouses and family budgets, that between a pound and a pound and a half of bread was consumed on average each day. The following budget reflects the prominence of bread in the expenditure of labouring families.

Expenses (annual) of a family of eight in Banbury

	£	s	d
Bread (60 lb. per week)	27	6	0
Rent	2	12	0
Fuel	2	12	0
Other	2	12	0
	35	2	0

In this case, bread forms about three-quarters of total family expenditure. It is not untypical. Compare the following weekly budget:

Expenses (weekly) of a family of four in Seend (Wiltshire)

	£	s	d
Bread (8 lb. per day)		11	0
Butter		1	6
Other		1	6
		14	0[5]

Nor did the place of bread alter very significantly in the early nineteenth century. Cobbett calculated that a family of five, comprising 'a man, wife, and three children, one child big enough to work, one big enough to eat heartily, and one a baby', would require five pounds of bread a day.[6]

Even though other foods were important, bread remained the staple foodstuff in the absence of a cheap and filling alternative. The bread consumed was increasingly wheaten, white bread by the middle of the eighteenth century. In the 1760s Charles Smith estimated that out of a population of about 6 million in England and Wales, 3,750,000 were wheat eaters, 880,000 ate rye, 739,000 ate barley, and 633,000 oats.[7] The consumption of wheaten bread was growing during the course of the eighteenth century and by the middle of the eighteenth century a degree of status had become attached to its consumption in many parts of England. Bakers and millers encouraged its sale because a higher profit could be obtained and coarser mixtures were regarded with suspicion. There was continuous demand from consumers for both finer and whiter bread during the century, the fashion being set by metropolitan tastes, where paradoxically, and to the despair of philanthropists and others, the whitest bread was consumed in the poorest areas, such as London's notorious 'rookeries'. Indeed the taste for whiter bread had developed so far that it was often adulterated with alum to whiten it for popular consumption. By the end of the eighteenth century, the prevailing view in the metropolitan area and much of southern England was that wheaten bread was the 'staff of life'.

Attempts to persuade the poor to eat other mixtures of grains or other foods in periods of scarcity were usually met with widespread consumer resistance. Eden reported that in 1796, a season of very high prices for wheat, attempts had been made to introduce barley bread into Gloucestershire, but that labourers could not be persuaded to abandon their normal practice of purchasing the finest wheaten bread. Arthur Young commented that labourers who had become accustomed to wheaten bread could no longer tolerate coarser varieties:

> In the East of England I have been very generally assured, by the labourers who work the hardest, that they prefer the finest bread, not because most pleasant, but most contrary to a lax habit of body, which at once prevents all strong labour. The quality of the bread that is eaten by those who have meat, and perhaps porter and port, is of very little consequence indeed: but to the hardworking man, who nearly lives on it, the case is abundantly different.[8]

By the eighteenth century England possessed a highly developed trade in foodstuffs, of which the grain trade was easily the most important. In normal years the total grain consumption of the country was estimated at about one quarter (28 lb.) per person per year. Until the 1750s, England was a net exporter of grain, but from the mid-century domestic production had to be supplemented by a growing quantity of imports as population growth began to outstrip supply, especially in years of harvest failure. Between 1775 and 1786 the annual average quantity of wheat imported was 180,000 quarters, representing about 2.5 per cent of total requirements. During the next decade, the figure had risen to 325,000 quarters, and reached 700,000 quarters in the decade 1799–1810.

As well as population growth, which made an insufficient harvest more likely, an increasing urban population was more and more dependent upon a market economy to supply them with food. During the course of the eighteenth century the chain between consumer and food producer became steadily more specialized and attenuated. From at least the Tudor period London's large urban population was stimulating a highly developed trade in foodstuffs in the home counties. By the eighteenth century the capital's supply network for grain embraced much of southern England and reached even further afield for more specialized produce. Existing manufacturing populations, such as the Cornish tinners and the cloth workers of East Anglia and the West Country, like the growing commercial cities and towns, were already dependent upon a relatively complex supply network to provide them with basic foodstuffs. With the growth of commerce and industry, especially in the latter half of the eighteenth century and the early nineteenth century, larger sections of the population became totally dependent upon an efficient marketing system to keep them supplied. Relatively few people in the eighteenth century actually produced grain for their own consumption, most were dependent upon buying grain, flour, or meal from dealers. Grain might be taken to a professional miller or to a manorial mill for turning into flour, and already in many areas, home-baking had largely ceased. Large and small towns, as well as the bigger villages, were increasingly dependent on the supply of bread from professional bakers.

Prior to the Napoleonic period the years 1766–7 were to give rise to one of the largest waves of disturbances to occur in England in modern times. The context was one of sharply rising prices brought about by poor harvests. Prices had been rising since 1763 and there were signs of disquiet as early as January 1766, when the Riot Act had to be used to disperse a mob in the West Country port of Lyme. Fearful of further disorder, the government ordered a restriction upon the export of grain on 26 February. This was to run until 26 August. Unfortunately, the harvest of 1766 also proved gravely disappointing.

The main wave of disturbances began at the end of July in the cloth towns of south Devon. At Honiton the poor seized bags of corn and sold them in the market place for 5s. 6d. a bushel, considerably below the prevailing price, but gave the money and the bags back to the owners when the selling had been finished. Disturbances then occurred at Ottery, Tipton, and Sidbury, spreading out to Lyme, Crediton, Exeter, and Barnstaple. In August the disturbances reached Newbury in Berkshire. On 7 August, the market place was invaded by 'a great number of poor people' who opened sacks of corn and scattered the contents about. They also took butter, cheese, meat, and bacon out of the shops and threw it into the streets. This demonstration of popular anger led the dealers to promise a reduction in the price of bread. The mob, however, continued its work at some neighbouring mills where flour was thrown into the river, and damage was estimated at £1,000.

There was then a lull in food riots which lasted until early September, when there were at least eighteen disturbances in various parts of the country. At Exeter and Stourbridge, the dealers in wheat and other food-stuffs were forced to reduce their prices. Disturbances spread to Bath, Tetbury, Malmesbury, and into the west Midlands at Kidderminster, Bewdley, Ludlow, and Wolverhampton. In the south, the riots spread out from the West Country to Trowbridge, Salisbury, and to the Thames Valley at Lechlade, Oxford, and Reading. The riots continued into October with at least forty separate incidents in that month alone. The majority of the disturbances occurred in the south-western, southern, and Midland counties. London and the south-east were relatively free from disturbances, as was the north, though there were disturbances in White-haven, Carlisle, and Berwick.

The majority of the disturbances were over by the end of October, but there were a few more in November, with riots at Bristol, Ludlow, Chelmsford, and Birmingham.[9] These disturbances also marked the begin-ning of a period of generally higher prices which were to reach their peak in the Napoleonic Wars. Although there were some small outbreaks of food rioting in 1772–3 and 1783, the years up to the outbreak of war with France in 1793 were not particularly eventful in terms of harvests and prices.

In fact it was a relatively low year for prices, 1792, which produced a small crop of food riots and a rather disproportionate response on the part of the authorities. At Nottingham in May 1792 'a great number of persons assembled and destroyed a large quantity of Butcher's meat, alleging . . . that the price was too high'. The disturbance was suppressed only when the military was called in. A few days later the soldiers had to be used again, when they fired at and attacked a number of journeymen shoemakers who were demanding higher wages. Disturbances about the price of provisions also spread to Leicester, where 'a number of disorderly persons' broke the windows of those dealers who were objects of popular dislike. Food riots also broke out at Leeds and Yarmouth. At Leeds the principal rioters were colliers, supported by a crowd of women and boys, and were sufficiently resolute to prevent the constables from dispersing them. At Yarmouth, in late October the Mayor was attacked by a mob when he sought to quell the disturbances. There were also fears of disturb-ances in autumn 1792 at Sheffield, Northampton, and Norwich. At the last, the Mayor, sheriffs, and aldermen petitioned the King to end the export of grain which they blamed for raising prices on the markets of

East Anglia. Parson Woodforde, at Weston Longville Parsonage, near Norwich, reflected a general atmosphere of tension which affected many sections of English society in the autumn of 1792, with rumours of riots and of mobs gathering.[10] But in spite of these rumours and anxieties, the total number of food riots in 1792 was very small. Whatever else was exciting the public imagination with the rapid progress of popular radicalism at home and abroad and the publication of the second part of Thomas Paine's *The Right of Man* in 1792, it was not a particularly severe year in terms of prices, nor were the disturbances which took place very significant in their own right.

A few food disturbances occurred in 1793. Cornwall was again affected by a temporary scarcity, and in February bodies of miners entered the towns in search of grain which they believed to be concealed in readiness for export. At Wadebridge they discovered 2,500 bushels in store which they forced the owners to sell at reduced prices, and at Looe they prevented 6,000 bushels from being exported. On 7 May there was a report that miners had come into Falmouth and forced the Mayor to let them have grain at 16s. a sack. Elsewhere there were disturbances about the price of butter. In Liverpool soldiers and workmen seized a quantity of butter, 'for which they would pay no more than 6d. per pound'. There was also a serious disturbance in the Sheffield butter market, where the dealers were driven away and the butter 'trodden under foot because they asked fifteen pence a pound for it'.

The period after 1793, however, witnessed a series of harvest failures and waves of food rioting which make it perhaps the most important concentration of this kind of disturbance in the whole period. The dislocation caused by the outbreak of war with France in 1793 and the continuance of hostilities with only short breaks until 1815 led to a certain amount of disruption for the overseas corn trade. Although England remained a marginal importer, except in very bad years, the inability to obtain sufficient supplies, or to obtain them without difficulty undoubtedly had its effect upon price levels throughout the wartime period. With demand for bread relatively inelastic, a shortfall in the domestic harvest or in the small quantities of imports usually required, could produce quite disproportionate rises in the price of foodstuffs. War, too, imposed additional demands upon the supply network, grain being required for armies overseas or for garrison troops in the country itself, which could easily distort local markets and interrupt normal channels of supply between one area and another.

There were four major outbreaks of food disturbances in this period, and they all occurred in periods of harvest failure and high prices. These were 1795–6, 1800–1, 1810–13 and 1816–18.[11] The shortage of 1795–6 started with the harvest of 1794 which was about 25 per cent below average, and as a result prices began to rise sharply in the pre-harvest months of 1795. By July wheat had reached an average of 108s. per quarter. The harvest of 1795 was also deficient, with the result that high prices were maintained through the winter of 1795–6, reaching a peak in the spring of 1796, when heavy imports of foreign grain broke the price spiral. It is this crisis which Professor Williams has called the 'English *crise des subsistances*'; while E. P. Thompson has described 1795 as the 'climactic' year for food riots in England.[12] The harvest was conservatively estimated to be between a third and a quarter below average. As early as February fears were expressed from Lancashire that 'the stock of wheat will be consumed, if not assisted from abroad, by the time the new comes to market or before'. A correspondent to the Home Secretary warned that 'want and war will accord ill with each other.'[13]

Table 2.1 Average price of wheat in England and Wales 1720–1818 in shillings per Winchester quarter

	s.	d.		s.	d.		s.	d.
1792	43	0	1801	119	6	1810	106	5
1793	49	3	1802	69	10	1811	95	3
1794	52	3	1803	58	10	1812	126	6
1795	75	2	1804	62	3	1813	109	9
1796	78	7	1805	89	9	1814	74	4
1797	53	9	1806	79	1	1815	65	7
1798	51	10	1807	75	4	1816	78	6
1799	69	0	1808	84	4	1817	96	11
1800	113	10	1809	97	4	1818	86	3

Source: B. R. Mitchell and Phyllis Deane, *Abstract of British Historical Statistics*, Cambridge, 1962, 488–9.

The scarcity of 1795–6 witnessed the greatest number of disturbances since 1766–7. There were at least eighty serious incidents, the great majority concentrated in 1795. The first disturbances began in the south-west in the spring of that year, but rapidly spread throughout the country reaching a peak in July 1795. Disturbances broke out in many small ports and market towns in southern England and East Anglia, spreading through the Midlands with disturbances at Oxford, Nuneaton, Nottingham, and Coventry. Further north, Sheffield, Knottingley, Castleford, Halifax, and surrounding areas were affected, whilst the disturbances also affected Darlington, Durham, Newcastle, and much of the north-west.

Disturbances tailed off a little during the winter of 1795–6, but there were riots at Ludlow in November and 1796 saw renewed rioting in Cornwall, Yorkshire, and the Midlands. At Truro in April some 3,000 miners had to be dispersed by the sheriff and six companies of Worcester militia, which charged the mob with fixed bayonets. By the summer of 1796, however, the disturbances had virtually come to an end,

Three years of ordinary harvests and moderate prices were ended by the harvest of 1799, which was between 25 and 40 per cent below average. By December 1799 the average price of wheat was almost 94s. per quarter; by May 1800 it had reached 120s. A further poor harvest in 1800 pushed prices still higher, reaching 140s. per quarter in January 1801. Before foreign imports could have their effect the price of wheat reached its highest level for the whole period, 156s. per quarter in March 1801. This period of shortage has received less attention than the earlier one, but contemporary evidence suggests that it was severely felt. Pellew in his *Life of Lord Sidmouth* wrote that 'a few days of rain in September 1800 produced consequences for which Pitt confessed he could see no adequate remedy and compared with which, he considered the great question of peace or war was not half so formidable'.[14]

The averages conceal the sharpness of the rise in prices at the local level. Not only corn but also other provisions rose in price; as consumers shifted from wheat to alternatives, they were similarly affected by bad weather. In Lancashire, wheat which had sold for 9s. a bushel in 1798 reached 18s. in 1800. Potatoes doubled in price from 1s. 6d. per stone in 1798 to 3s. 0d. in 1800. Even by the end of 1799 this manufacturing district was feeling the effects of the scarcity. The Rev. Richard Perryn said that he believed the Wigan area would have starved but for supplies of foreign wheat and American flour which came into the country during 1799.[15] Once again the rise in prices led to serious disturbances. As early as November 1799, 'a number of people, consisting principally of women', went to Huddersfield from the neighbouring villages and seized all the corn brought into market. In spring 1800 there were numerous instances of unrest which failed to break out into open rioting, either through the energies of local magistrates or the calming effect of private philanthropy. On the whole, the pre-harvest months were relatively undisturbed in 1800, but the autumn proved quite the opposite. A rash of riots broke out in September and October 1800, many of them focused upon the evils of middlemen. The south and Midlands were the most affected, and there were serious riots at Nuneaton, Nottingham, Banbury, Oxford, and Birmingham. The disturbances began to die away in the winter months of 1800–1 but there were renewed incidents in April 1801, mainly in the West Country. The disturbances occurred in many parts of Cornwall, with Launceston and St Austell the most affected. At the latter a crowd of women and tinners went around the neighbouring farms with a written paper in one hand and a rope in the other. If the farmers hesitated to sign the paper, which pledged them to sell their corn at a reduced price, the rope was fastened about their necks and they were terrified into signing. By the end of April 1801, however, the worst of the riots were over.

Wheat prices remained moderate for the next eight years, but in 1809 and the three subsequent years crops failed. Wheat prices exceeded 100s.

per quarter every week from October 1811 until the scarcity ended in 1813. By August 1812 wheat had reached 155s. per quarter. It was also a time of acute commercial distress and disturbances broke out against machinery as well as against the price of food. During the shortage there were not only at least twenty-nine food disturbances, there was also the first wave of Luddite outbreaks.

A number of incidents stand out as being typical of the kind of food rioting found earlier. The biggest group of riots occurred in 1812. In one month alone, April, there were food riots at Bristol, Sheffield, Birmingham, Carlisle, Oldham, Manchester, Rochdale, Stockport, Macclesfield, and Stockport. Later in the year, there were market disturbances at Wakefield, Nottingham, and Loughborough. At Carlisle, the mob seized grain and potatoes from Liverpool dealers who were taking it out of the country, while at Macclesfield the crowd threw into the street vegetables which they considered too highly priced. When one of the leaders was arrested the crowd released him and returned to the market-place, where they attacked provision shops, broke down windows and doors, and threw the goods into the street. Disturbances also broke out in the West Country with mobs going into the market towns or around the farms demanding grain; Truro, Barnstaple, Falmouth, and Plymouth were the scenes of the most serious disturbances.

The last major wave of food disturbances to affect England occurred in the years 1816–18. As in 1810–13 there was some overlap with the industrial troubles (Luddism). The background was one of trade depression, with subsequent distress among the workmen, but also poor harvests in 1816 and 1817. Prices had almost fallen to pre-war levels in 1815, but in the months before the harvest in 1816 they began to rise rapidly causing disturbances in a number of places, especially in East Anglia. A cold, wet summer produced a harvest which was deficient in both quantity and quality. The result was more disturbances as prices rose sharply in the winter of 1816–17 and intermittent disturbances occurred until 1818.

The most serious incidents took place in East Anglia, centred on the Isle of Ely, but extending into Suffolk. A spate of fires and threatening letters were reported, as well as nightly gatherings of the labourers. Rioters at Littleport and Downham mobbed the magistrates, demanding higher wages and lower prices; they split up into several parties and scattered through the towns and villages of the neighbourhood with similar demands. The crowds were occasionally armed with staves studded with spikes and in one or two instances they had muskets and bayonets. There were several clashes with the local yeomanry, militia, or regular dragoons, and at Littleport, two of the rioters were killed and seventy-five taken prisoner. So alarmed was the Government that it tried the prisoners by Special Commission: twenty-four were capitally convicted, of whom five were eventually executed, whilst the others were transported or imprisoned in Ely.[16] Disturbances also broke out at Frome, Stockport, Bolton, Coventry, Hinckley, and Birmingham. At Bridport on 6 May 2,000 of the 'manufacturing poor' assembled 'in consequence of the advance in the price of bread' and also lack of employment. The crowd bore a quartern loaf on the end of a pole and smashed the windows of the principal bakers and millers before being dispersed by an organized body of inhabitants. At the end of the year there were more disturbances, with mobs threatening the bakers at Towcester and Sheffield. A trickle of minor food disturbances occurred in 1817 and 1818 whilst prices still remained high, and in March 1817 there were disturbances amongst the miners at Radstock and at Maryport in Cumberland. The next autumn there were disturbances amongst the colliers at Whitehaven, but thereafter rapidly improving prospects in trade and harvests virtually brought an end to the riots.

Despite high prices the food riots of this period rarely denoted a real subsistence crisis, but rather a consumer reaction to prices which were considered to be 'unfair'. Unfortunately evidence of the prices at which food was resold or to which it was reduced is only available in a small number of detailed reports of food disturbances. From these, however, it appears that the 'fair' price for food was by no means constant. In 1795 the lowest price at which wheat was resold was 42s. a quarter (Seaford), which corresponded to the lowest average for the past decade, that of the immediate pre-war year, 1792. By 1800, however, wheat was being resold and reduced to prices of between 80s. a quarter (Oxford) and 100s. a quarter (Leicester). Here even the 'fair' prices were higher than anything previously experienced. The prices at which bread was demanded also show an increase: in 1795 the quartern load was demanded at 9d. (Hadstock) but for 1s. in 1800 (Banbury). Similarly meat, which was resold at 4d. a pound in 1795 (Guildford, Seaford, and Handborough) was fixed in 1800 from 5d. a pound (Oxford) to 7d. a pound (Nuneaton). Butter, too, showed an increase in the 'fair' price, from 8d. a pound in 1795 (Wells) to 1s. a pound in 1800 (Oxford). From this evidence, albeit fragmentary, it appears that the 'fair' price was not a fixed one, deriving from some standard in the past, but one which was dictated by local circumstances and the conditions of the market in each year.

The interpretation of these disturbances as manifestations of general 'consumer consciousness' is borne out by considering how many of them were 'grocery' riots, concerned not only with the price of grain, flour, or bread, but also of other foodstuffs. Commodities included: meat (Redruth, St Austell: 1766; Wisbech, Coventry, Portsea: 1795; Oxford, Nuneaton: 1800, Brandon: 1816); cheese (Exeter, Coventry, Oxford: 1766; Seaford: 1795; Nuneaton, London: 1800); butter (Stourbridge, Kidderminster: 1767; Bury St Edmunds: 1772; Liverpool: 1793; Wells, Aylesbury, Deddington: 1795; Oxford, Banbury: 1800; Carlisle: 1812); and potatoes

(Manchester: 1757; Truro: 1766; Hull: 1795; Manchester, Carlisle: 1812; Bideford: 1816). Other price-fixing riots involved the price of green vegetables, bacon, malt, and even candles and soap. These were usually treated in the same way as grain or bread, with attempts to regulate the price and the spoiling of the goods if this was not complied with. Although disturbances concerning the price of grain, flour, and bread remained the most common, 'grocery' disturbances were an increasing proportion of the total. Looking at the disturbances after 1789 it can be seen that about half of them were solely or partly concerned with other commodities than bread or bread grains.

There are clear indications of a geographical shift in the location of food riots between the seventeenth and early nineteenth centuries. In the seventeenth century food riots were common in East Anglia, the Thames valley, and the cloth towns of the West Country. This pattern remained well into the eighteenth century, for relatively few disturbances took place in northern districts and food rioting was largely a southern phenomenon. The typical food riot took place in small market towns or ports of southern England. By 1800–1, however, the majority of disturbances took place in the manufacturing areas of the Midlands and the north. This pattern was confirmed in the riots of 1810–13, when the centres of disturbances were the manufacturing towns of the Midlands, mainly Birmingham and Nottingham, the cotton towns of Lancashire around Manchester, and the mining towns on the Yorkshire coalfield. The disturbances of 1816 occurred in several parts of the country, but the majority again occurred in the Midlands and north, though the centres of production and transportation in East Anglia and the small ports were also disturbed.[17]

As we have seen, the food disturbances of these years were frequently composed of a typical cross-section of the local population, often including members of manufacturing groups. Yet, in comparison with France, one of the most interesting characteristics is the relatively smaller part played by agricultural labourers. Rudé has argued that in French country riots of the mid-eighteenth century the principle participants were wine-growers and farm labourers, whereas in England groups of workmen or clearly identified categories, such as the 'poor', are usually cited by contemporaries as being responsible.[18] E. P. Thompson has also confirmed this view, but with the qualification that farm labourers did become involved in disturbances where other groups gave a lead.[19] Settled farm labourers may well have been affected by greater deference towards superiors than the inhabitants of the local market town or pit village. Probably more important, however, they were also less dependent upon the market-place to provide them with food. Living on the land they had far less reason to fear absolute scarcity than their urban compatriots. There is evidence that in times of scarcity farmers withheld corn from market, whether to use as seed, for fear of disorder, or simply to profit from the rise in price, but it meant that country areas were rarely short of grain. Agricultural workers therefore had easier access to grain in times of shortage; there were several reports from harassed urban magistrates in 1795–6 that farmers were selling off what little grain was available for sale at artificially low prices to their labourers. Even before the introduction of the Speenhamland system in 1795, the practice of subsidizing or supplementing wages was quite common in the southern counties.[20] With the spread of the practice of fixing poor relief in relation to the current price of bread or wheat, agricultural workers were effectively cushioned from fluctuations in food prices.

The major exception to the pattern in which farmworkers played little part in food rioting is the outbreak of disturbances in East Anglia in the spring of 1816, which centred upon Ely, Littleport, and Downham. In this area, however, agricultural change had created a large population of wage-labourers, living in populous 'open' parishes. In East Anglia the position of agricultural labourers most closely resembled that of those engaged in manufacturing, and it is significant that in 1816 they combined demands for a reduction in food prices with ones for higher wages. Significantly, in the great wave of disturbances which spread over southern England in 1830–2 there were virtually no instances of food rioting outside the south-west.

Thus the south-west was the last bastion of food rioting in England. As late as 1867 there were a number of food disturbances in Teignmouth and Exeter, whereas in the rest of the country food rioting had by then given way to other forms of protest and action.[21] Although food rioting remained an important part of popular protest in many parts of Europe well into the twentieth century, it had largely died out in England by the middle of the nineteenth.

Notes

1   Rudé, 1964, 63–8.
2   Tilley, 1969, 16–19.
3   Walter and Wrightson, 1976, 26.
4   Stevenson, 1979, 91–4; Charlesworth, 1983, 80–118.
5   Eden, 1966, II 586, III 796.
6   Cobbett, 1967, 305–6.
7   Smith, 1766, 140, 182–5.
8   Young, 1796, 455.
9   Charlesworth, 1983, 88–92; Shelton, 1973, 21–49.
10 Beresford, 1967, 423–4, 427.
11 Stevenson, 1974, 33–74; Charlesworth, 1983, 97–106.
12 G. A. Williams, 1968, 101; E. P. Thompson, 1968, 73.
13 Dodd, 1965, 96; John Rylands Library, R. 926 (Dundas Papers), f. 13: Devagnes to Dundas, 10 February 1795.
14 Pellew, 1847, I 270.

15 Dodd, 1965, 103.
16 For the fullest descriptions of these disturbances, see Peacock, 1965.
17 Charlesworth, 1983, 104–7.
18 Rudé, 1964, 45.
19 E. P. Thompson, 1971, 119.
20 Bohstedt, 1983, 169–70; Bawn, 1984, 12–20.
21 Charlesworth, 1983, 71.

3

'Rural war': the life and times of Captain Swing

G. E. Mingay

Between 1 June 1830 and 3 September 1831 the most recent historians of the Swing riots have enumerated the occurrence of nearly 1,500 disturbances, ranging from the sending of threatening letters to arson, machine breaking, and rioting of various descriptions.[1] This widespread and alarming upsurge of unrest on the part of agricultural labourers was by far the greatest in modern English history and, moreover, it had no successor: it was, truly, the 'Last Labourers' Revolt'.

More generally the disturbances have been dubbed the 'Swing Riots'. It is interesting that in some counties the term 'swing' or 'swingel' was used for the part of the flail that struck the corn; and many of the riots were set off by the threat posed by the recently-introduced threshing machine to the men's winter employment of threshing the corn by hand with the flail. Captain Swing as an individual almost certainly never existed, though 'strangers', 'well-dressed individuals', and 'gentlemanly-looking men' were reported to have been seen at places where fires had broken out. The labourers who penned bloodcurdling 'Swing letters' seized upon the name as a sufficiently impressive subscription, and some may well have believed in his existence. But in the welter of scattered and varied incidents there is little sign of any plan on a national scale or a central directing hand. There must have been some degree of local organization, however, and it is significant that many outbreaks can be traced as developing along the network of main roads in southern and eastern England. The role of the larger communities along these main roads may well have been crucial. They were more likely to house radical individuals and societies, and also the Dissenting Chapels, whose preachers sometimes acted as spokesmen for the rioters; while radical craftsmen and others were often the leading spirits of local disturbances, their language strongly tinged by that of Cobbett's writings. The main roads, it has been argued, served to spread radical ideas by providing easy access to the literature and news emanating from London as well as personal contact with radical leaders.[2]

The influence of the roads on the geographical pattern of incidents was made effective also by the role of coachmen, travellers, carriers, drovers, and tramps in spreading news of incidents recently occurring in places they had come from or passed through. The news was no doubt magnified in the telling, and may have served as the spark which set alight the impatient tinder of restless men. There was certainly a good deal of imitation, one type of action giving rise to similar ones across a neighbourhood. In West Sussex, for instance, the disturbances of mid-November 1830 came some ten or eleven weeks after the early outbreaks in Kent: 'we know what they have done in Kent', the rioters at Pulborough said. Tidings of the riots were spread also by newspaper reports, by letters, and by inflammatory messages carried along the roads, such as the 'luridly-phrased' one from a 'Johnny Bonny' borne by an 'itinerant Irishman, who vends leather straps', arrested at Bishop's Stortford.[3]

The number of 1,500 disturbances may somewhat exaggerate the extent of the unrest since the total includes every town, village, or farm where an incident occurred, though often the same gang of rioters would go from place to place, gathering recruits (sometimes unwilling ones) and leaving behind a trail of smashed threshing machines. Further, a substantial element consisted of smugglers, poachers, and other 'natural rebels', men accustomed to breaking the law, who might well stimulate into action the normally peaceable labourers, craftsmen, and small farmers. Whatever the true strength of the unrest (and over 2,000 were ultimately charged with offences) there is no doubt about its geographical concentration. Five southern counties, Hampshire, Wiltshire, Berkshire, Kent, and Sussex, between them accounted for 880 incidents, well over half the total. Another six counties, Norfolk and Suffolk, together with Essex, Buckinghamshire, Dorset, and Gloucestershire, contributed another 292; only 129 incidents were noted in thirteen midland and northern counties, none at all in Northumberland, Durham, Westmorland, or Cumberland.[4]

The rioters were thus essentially a phenomenon of southern and eastern England. Twenty years after Swing, James Caird, the eminent Victorian agriculturist, remarked on the division between the northern half of the country, where the labourers were relatively well paid, and the southern half, where the wages were on average as much as 27 per cent lower. His line dividing the high-wage and low-wage areas ran westwards from the Wash through the middle of Leicestershire, along the boundary between Staffordshire and Worcestershire, and then turned northwards through Shropshire to end on the estuary of the Dee.[5] In drawing this distinction Caird pointed to a significant influence on agricultural pay – the effect of industry in putting a floor under farm wages. In southern England, with the outstanding exception of London, there were no industrial centres large enough to exert the same ameliorating influence, and in the more purely agricultural districts the cash wages could sink to the eight, seven, or even six shillings a week paid in parts of the West Country, the south Midlands, and East Anglia.

Pressure of numbers was one of the other factors helping to keep wages down in the southern half of England. There was certainly a degree of mobility, especially seasonal movement, as gangs of men moved round a circuit of farms competing with itinerant Irish, Welsh, or Scots for the relatively well-paid harvest work. And people did move more permanently, as evidence of marriage registers and of townspeople's places of birth makes clear. Nevertheless, in 1830 rural out-migration was not yet on a sufficient scale to compensate for the effects of the high birthrate and the decline or disappearance of former sources of employment, such as the old textile trades in East Anglia and the wealden iron industry of Kent and Sussex and the Forest of Dean. By 1830 the ancient prosperity of the East Anglian cloth towns lingered on only in the memory of the older inhabitants. For example, in Halstead, on the Essex–Suffolk border, only four of the formerly numerous clothiers were still in business in 1791, and by 1800 even these survivors had given up; over 2,000 of the town's 3,300 inhabitants were thrown upon the charity of the parish. Although migration of the rural poor occurred, it was beset with difficulties: the lack of nearby alternative employment and ignorance of conditions further afield; insufficient funds to meet the costs of looking for work; the encumbrance of large families; the hostility of the poor law authorities to migrants when relief was still based on the parish where the person was born or had worked for over a year.

There was frequently not so much a total lack of work as insufficient work. Under-employment was especially marked in arable areas. Corn growing required a large number of men, a village with 2,000 acres of arable employing some seventy or eighty men and boys on the land itself, together with those involved in milling and carrying, as well as men in other trades and local crafts serving the farmers. Such villages rarely had any large source of alternative employment, and as the number of inhabitants grew there were those who could find work only in the busy seasons like haymaking and harvesting, and who depended on the parish for all or most of the winter. Pastoral villages, and those with many smallholdings, saw less under-employment because there the farms were mainly family units employing few paid hands, and livestock needed continuous care the whole year round. Woodland districts had the advantage of much winter work in planting, thinning, and felling trees, in stripping bark, and cutting and transporting the wood, and there were often associated trades, the making of fencing, gates, hurdles, poles and posts, barrel staves, besoms, and the like. In such places fuel was cheap, acorns and mast could be gathered to feed the pigs, and labourers might live well. Over and over again Cobbett noted the advantages of wooded areas over corn ones: 'the more purely a corn country', he argued, 'the more miserable the labourers.'[6]

The fifteen years between the ending of the Wars and 1830 had not been good ones for the labourers. In the earlier part of the period the shortage of work was intensified not only by the rising population but also by the throwing on to the labour market of discharged soldiers and sailors and industrial workers displaced by the post-war depression. Prices, it is true, had fallen from the excessively high wartime levels – the 4 lb. loaf, a commodity vital to labouring families, fell from its peak of 1812 to nearly half the price by 1821–2. But the rest of the 1820s saw no further fall, and in 1830 bread was as dear as it had been in 1815, while in the interim wages had fallen substantially. Furthermore, for those families who relied entirely or partially on the parish, the changing attitudes of the authorities and new policies of poor relief had tended to work against them. Parishes tried to reduce the burden of poor rates by cutting back on relief, by making it more difficult to obtain, and by instituting schemes which degraded the pauper or attempted to deter the poor from seeking any relief at all. It is not surprising that a number of Swing incidents centred round unpopular overseers and hostility towards the workhouses. Some workhouses were destroyed, the property of overseers put to the torch, their dignity slighted and their persons maltreated. At Brede, near Battle in Sussex, an unfortunate Mr Abel, an assistant overseer, was unceremoniously wheeled out of the village in the parish cart, normally reserved for transporting paupers, and dumped across the boundary of the neighbouring parish. The spirit of emulation soon resulted in similar treatment of other obnoxious overseers in neighbouring parts of Sussex, the perpetrators including smugglers, whose more customary and nefarious activities were endemic on and near the Sussex coast. Further west, just across the border in Hampshire at Selborne and Headley, workhouses were demolished in 'a combined operation with threshing machines, tithes and overseers of the poor as its targets'.[7]

The unrest of the period was fed also by the widening of the social and material gap between the gentry and larger farmers and the small farmers and work-people. In the past many squires had felt a strong sense of obligation towards the inhabitants of villages where they had their seats and where their main concentrations of property were situated. They dipped into their pockets to support schools and local charities, to repair the churches, and sometimes to provide the services of a doctor or apothecary. They held roisterous fêtes on special occasions, responded to appeals from those who had suffered accidents, damage by fire, or losses of livestock, and they wrote letters on behalf of the untutored and, in an age of few and unstable banks, they kept their savings for them on trust at current rates of interest. Such social concern was not, in truth, very costly, but it helped maintain the squire's local popularity and brought him into closer contact with the villagers and their problems, and it contributed to an atmosphere of mutual interest and respect. This relationship, never consistent nor universal, seems to have declined as the villages grew larger, became more industrialized and more independent, and as an increasing number of landowners chose to spend their lives elsewhere and became absentees.

The Game Laws, too, drove a wedge between landowners and villagers. The preservation of game birds was a nuisance and source of loss to the farmers, while the existence of preserves offered a powerful temptation to gangs of commercial poachers and village youths alike. From the beginning of the new century the Game Laws mounted in severity, the Act of 1803 making resistance to arrest punishable by death, and that of 1817 awarding seven years' transportation to armed poachers caught at night. Only in 1828 did some relaxation begin, the Act of that year reserving transportation for the third offence, with the first and second offences punishable by three months' and six months' imprisonment respectively. Commitments for poaching rose sharply in the four years preceding 1830, when the annual average reached 281, indicating not only the ineffectiveness of repressive laws but also the mounting disregard of the poor for the principle of private property. It has to be remembered, however, that much of the poaching was the work not of the labourer desperate to feed a hungry family but rather that of a young man seeking a little excitement to brighten a dull bucolic existence, and especially the depredations of organized gangs who had the profitable London market for game in view.[8]

The high agricultural prices and swelling profits of the Napoleonic Wars had fostered a breed of large-scale tenant farmers, men who rented additional farms in neighbouring parishes and installed their sons or bailiffs in the vacant farmhouses to supervise their extended operations. The living standards of these monopolizing farmers escalated with their revenues. Contemporaries complained of their airs and affectations, their houses and carriages which aped those of the gentry, their fine furniture, pianofortes, and services of silver, their port laid down by the pipe, their sons who went off to study under dancing instructors and fencing masters, and their daughters whose finery and elegance made them indistinguishable from the daughters of a duchess. Some of these great farmers fell on hard times when prices tumbled at the end of the Wars and credit was severely restricted, but many survived, and the change in manners was one of the many vexations voiced by Cobbett in his journeys of the early 1820s. Successful farmers no longer suffered the company of their farm servants at the dinner table or even in the kitchen, but banished them to outhouses; or they dispensed with annual hirings and instead engaged day labourers who lived out in cottages. It may be, as Cobbett fulminated, that thereby money was saved, for work-people could no longer be fed in the farmhouse on the pitiful sums paid them in wages.[9] However, in most districts the really big farmer was rare or unknown, and it is evident that in the Swing episode there were many occasions when farmers, presumably the smaller ones, felt sympathy with the rioters, encouraged them, and in some instances themselves took an active part in the disturbances.

In many a village the labourer looked in vain for a kind face among the superior classes of gentry, parsons, professional men, and larger farmers. The parsons, often at this time magistrates and active in the pursuit of law breakers, were not infrequently the particular object of the men's ire. The labourers joined to demand a reduction of the parson's tithes, a move often directly or indirectly supported by the farmers. The men understood, or seem to have been persuaded, that farmers could not be expected to pay higher wages unless their outgoings in rents and tithes were reduced. A Mr Cobbold, vicar of Selborne, recent successor to the celebrated Gilbert White, was told by the men that he should reduce his tithes by a half: 'we think £300 a year quite enough for you . . . £6 a week is quite enough.' At Edingthorpe in Norfolk the rector was confronted not by the labourers but by an abusive deputation of farmers, who threatened to take matters into their own hands, their leader saying that the rector 'should have nothing at all if they did not please'. Pressure on the clergy was intensified when farmers boldly declared to the rioters that higher wages would not be paid unless the tithes went down. At Haddiscoe, also in Norfolk, the Rev. Thomas Elliston was besieged in the Crown Inn, where he had gone to collect his tithes, by 'an assembly of persons' carrying a red flag and blowing a horn, who said 'that they needed a reduction of the tithes, so that their masters might pay them more wages'.[10]

How far the radical agitation of the years preceding 1830 influenced the Swing revolt is difficult to determine. Many of the labourers were illiterate or nearly so, and the reading of newspapers or broadsides was uncommon among them. But in the larger villages there were tradesmen and crafts-men, persons of superior education and knowledge, shoemakers, in par-ticular, being notorious for their radical leanings. It is interesting that a number of craftsmen were arrested in the course of the riots, and the judges were evidently alarmed and nonplussed that persons of their status, economic independence, and higher understanding should have involved themselves in mindless damage to property and menaces to magistrates, parsons, and other members of the governing class. William Oakley and Alfred Darling were two of three men convicted and reserved for execution in the trials at Reading, but later reprieved. Darling was a blacksmith, found guilty on charges of demanding money, and Oakley, who had placed himself at the head of a mob and exacted £5 from the magistrates at Hungerford, was told by the judge that, as a carpenter, he had no business to mix himself up in these transactions.[11]

41

Whether it was his business or not, it is easy to imagine men of the stamp of Oakley taking the lead in a situation where the ordinary labourer might find a face-to-face confrontation with magistrates unnerving. Craftsmen of radical sympathies were, as we have noted, among the leaders of some of the rioters, and their recorded demands and statements had a Cobbett-like ring about them. Such radicals may have helped evoke unrest by recounting from the newspapers word of such events as Peterloo or the more recent demand for reform of Parliament and the July 1830 revolution in France. The agitation for Parliamentary reform reached a peak in London in early November 1830, and it is striking that the same month saw the most numerous and sustained Swing outbursts in the countryside. Between 15 November and the end of the month Swing incidents occurred at no fewer than 500 places spread over a very large area, but mainly concentrated in southern counties stretching from Kent in the east to Wiltshire and Gloucestershire in the west; almost 250 of the incidents took place on the four days 21–4 November.[12]

Perhaps, too, the labourers had had explained to them the schemes of land reform and home colonization which had been put forward since the time of Thomas Spence and Arthur Young; or had heard read aloud in a public house the violent verbal assaults of Cobbett on pernicious fund-lords and malevolent tax-eaters. But it is less easy to imagine simple labourers, who may never in their lives have journeyed further than the nearest market town, finding much stimulus in these matters. Manchester and Paris were as remote to these men as Timbuctoo, land reform an unreal panacea of impractical idealists, and Cobbett's fiery words largely incomprehensible and irrelevant. Cobbett in person, however, may have had some influence. The disturbances in Sussex began, the authorities stated, soon after 'a lecture lately given here (at Battle) publicly by a person named Cobbett'. And after the riots, Thomas Goodman, a farm labourer of 18 condemned to death for setting five fires near Battle, saved his life by declaring in prison that the idea had been put into his head by hearing Cobbett lecture. 'i believe that there never would bean any fires or mob in Battle nor maney other places if he never had given aney lactures at all', the lad was reported to have said. Cobbett strongly denied the implication of the confession, denouncing the statement as a fraud, which in his eyes was the more likely since it had been taken down by a parson, and moreover a parson who had come twenty miles to solicit it.[13]

Cobbett also pointed out that the fires had begun, not in Sussex, but in east Kent, where he had not been for years, while those in west Kent started three months before he went there. Whatever his personal influence, readers of his *Political Register* could have been in no doubt how he viewed the plight of the country – 'the labouring people in a state of half-starvation' – and how he predicted the outbreaks. 'A sufficiency of food and raiment' was looked upon by the countryman as his inheritance, stated Cobbett. 'Never, let what will happen, will these people lie down and starve quietly.' And when he wrote subsequently of the effectiveness of the labourers' actions – that they had produced an improvement in the labourers' lot, and that the terror of the fires had unquestionably brought down the tithes – the government pounced, though unsuccessfully, the charge of seditious libel being rejected by the court.[14]

Nothing so far explains just why 1830 should have been the year when within six months burnt-out barns and stacks and remains of threshing machines scarred the farms of nearly a score of counties. It has to be pointed out, first, that some of the Swing kinds of disturbances – arson, robbery, destruction of machinery, attacks on unpopular figures – were not uncommon in the countryside and had featured in previous outbreaks, notably the East Anglian riots of 1816 and 1822. These riots, like Swing, were motivated in large part by low wages, hunger, and lack of work. But after they had been suppressed the countryside was never entirely quiet. Farmers still found their stacks set alight and livestock maimed, and some magistrates, parsons, and overseers found it unwise to venture out alone on dark nights. How far the continuing disquiet was due to the persisting distress which had sparked the uprising of 1816, and how far to individual grievances of men who thought themselves unfairly discharged, convicted, or refused relief, it is impossible to say. Certainly after 1816 there were continuing poverty, unemployment, and hunger, but events more immediate to the summer of 1830 seem to have provided the detonator necessary to set off a fresh and much greater explosion.

Farming conditions had deteriorated in the two years preceding the first Swing outbreaks. Cobbett claimed in May 1829 that farmers had then not been able to pay more that 60 per cent, on average, of their Lady-Day rents, and that trade in general was in a wretched state.[15] Bad harvests, certainly, marked both 1828 and 1829, and there were also severe outbreaks of disease among the livestock. The farmers were in difficulty, and some may have looked for reductions in their wage-bill at the very time when the price of bread, the labourers' staple, had risen. These conditions may also help to explain why some farmers encouraged the labourers in their protests and took a leading part in demands for reductions in rents and tithes.

But it would be wrong to put too much weight on economic, political, or social factors of a general kind in seeking the causes of the riots. Analysis of the incidents does not reveal any very clear or consistent pattern. For example, arson was most common in Kent, Sussex and Lincolnshire, and was relatively uncommon elsewhere; riots against tithes were heavily concentrated in Sussex, Norfolk, and Suffolk, but against the poor law in Kent and Sussex; no threshing machines were broken in Bedfordshire, Lincoln, or Surrey and only one each in Cambridgeshire,

Suffolk, and the Sussex weald; while the incidence of robbery and burglary associated with the riots was most marked in Hampshire, Wiltshire, and Berkshire. It seems that purely local influences operated more directly on the course of events. Riots broke out where there was large-scale arable farming, but also where there was not; where radical undercurrents were present and where they were absent; where the supposedly demoralizing Speenhamland type of bread-scale allowance to the poor was operated, where it was not, and where there were no allowances at all. In Kent riots broke out at Barham, where no Speenhamland allowances were given, and at Lenham where they were. At Tenterden the overseers turned to allowances only after the riots. None of these places could be considered centres of large-scale arable farming, but at Barham the farmers had persisted in using their threshing machines although the vestry had recommended their disuse, Lenham was notorious for unemployment, and Tenterden was a centre of dissent. The existence of dissenting sects was sometimes an indication of proneness to riot: Elham, for example, whence came some of the first machine breakers in east Kent, housed a colony of Bible Christians, as did Tenterden.[16]

Among other local factors which might be of importance were the behaviour and attitude of the villages' local 'aristocracy'. Church of England parsons might be unpopular, if only because of their tithes; and overseers, too, who had gone out of their way to humiliate and degrade those seeking parish relief. Both parsons and overseers might be farmers and find their stacks burnt down, and it seems that it was the farmers as a whole who bore the brunt of the labourers' activities. Two-thirds of the 202 cases of arson, where it has been possible to identify the victim, involved farmers, as against 36 involving landlords, justices, and gentry, 21 tradesmen, 12 parsons, and 9 overseers. Two out of every five of the 82 identified recipients of threatening letters were also farmers, against 19 who were parsons, 16 landlords, 12 tradesmen, and 2 overseers. And farmers must have suffered the most heavily in the breaking of threshing machines. Probably it was the larger gentlemen farmers, more akin to the lesser gentry in their incomes and style of living than to small working farmers, who were more likely to be victimized: reports from Berkshire spoke of 'the total want of feeling of the farmers towards the common labourers'. But perhaps the great majority of farmers, if not merely passive, were sympathetic allies in the labourers' cause.[17] At all events, it is perhaps unwise to read too much into the figures just quoted. The information is only partial: the victims of over a hundred – a third – of the cases of arson have not been identified, nor those of seventeen of the ninety-nine Swing letters. Further, there may well have been a strong accidental element in the choice of victims, depending on who was uppermost in the rioters' minds at the time, and whose stacks and threshing machines were most readily accessible.

Members of the landlord class, as we have seen, received a fair proportion of the rioters' attentions. Some, no doubt, had treated the men
with contempt and arrogance, some may have recently raised their rents,
turned labourers out of cottages and small farmers out of their holdings,
and some, as Justices, may have been heavy-handed in sentencing poachers, smugglers, thieves, vagrants, and the other perpetrators of rural crime.
However, when the riots began a number of magistrates showed considerable sympathy with the labourers. At the east Kent quarter sessions held
at Canterbury on 22 October 1830, the presiding magistrate, Sir Edward
Knatchbull, discharged seven prisoners with a caution and a mere three-
day prison sentence, expressing the hope that 'kindness and moderation'
would bring the offences to an end. In Norfolk, similarly, the North
Walsham magistrates issued a public notice recommending the farmers to
discontinue the use of threshing machines and to raise the wages of their
men to 10s. a week; it was believed, the magistrates said, that no severe
measures would be necessary if landowners and farmers would give 'proper
employment to the Poor'.[18]

Such moderation did not recommend itself to all magistrates, however,
and certainly not to the government, which reacted to the news from the
country by instructing magistrates to resist demands for wage increases
and reductions of rents and tithes 'when accompanied with violence and
Menace', and reminding them of their duty to 'maintain and uphold the
Rights of Property, of every Description, against violence and Aggres-
sion'.[19] And there were certainly landlords and magistrates who most
wholeheartedly agreed with the government's stand. Such a one was Sir
John Benett of Pyt House, Tisbury in Wiltshire. Benett, a Member for
his county and a well-known local figure, had already shown his disdain
for the labourers by asserting that he would pull down his cottages if
length of residence were to become a qualification for obtaining poor
relief. A large proportion of the inhabitants of Tisbury were already in
receipt of relief, and Lord Arundel, who lived there, described the poor
as 'more oppressed' and 'in greater misery as a whole than [in] any Parish
in the Kingdom'. On the morning of 25 November 1830 Benett was roused
by his steward with the news that rioters were approaching Pyt House.
He rode out to meet them and found some 400 labourers armed with
bludgeons and crowbars intent on destroying his threshing machines.
Benett's threats and appeals could not stay the rioters, who pelted him
with stones, broke into his barns, and destroyed two machines before a
troop of yeomen cavalry arrived on the scene. The first discharge of the
yeomanry's muskets with blank cartridges aimed above the mob's heads
merely produced laughter. The rioters retreated into the wood around Pyt
House and from there stoned the troops who responded with a fierce
onslaught, shooting one man dead and cutting off the fingers and opening
the skulls of several others. Twenty-five of the rioters were arrested. They

claimed later that 'the farmers were at the bottom of it: that they gave them beer and urged them to excesses'. The excesses drew their grim reward at the Special Commission which was held at Salisbury in the following January. Thirteen men were transported for seven years and one for fourteen years for breaking threshing machines on the day of the Pyt House affray.[20]

One other local cause which has been suggested for the riots is the effects of enclosures of common fields and common lands. The number of enclosures, however, had fallen away after the collapse of the high prices at the end of the Napoleonic Wars, and in any event were not at any time very numerous in the southern counties most affected by the Swing outbreaks. Kent, for example, had only some scattered enclosures affecting a mere 8,000 acres, and Sussex and Essex had only 41,000 and 42,000 acres affected respectively. Only three of the 1,475 incidents of 1830–1 could be ascribed directly to enclosure.[21] In fact the type of village most likely to spawn a riot was not a recently-enclosed one but rather one that was relatively populous (with a higher than average proportion of craftsmen and shopkeepers), less agricultural and a more important centre for trade and communications than more rustic places; it was likely to be relatively independent of the control of a squire or parson, and often had a strong Nonconformist influence.[22]

Lastly we must consider the significance of the threshing machine. The machine, as we have noted, reduced the labourer's employment at the very time of the year when other work was scarce. Attacks on threshing machines had been a feature of the earlier riots in East Anglia, and they seem to have been a major precipitating influence in those of 1830. After a scattering of threatening letters and fires in various places during the spring and summer of 1830, the riots began in earnest with the breaking of threshing machines at Lower Hardres, near Canterbury, on the night of 28 August, and at Newington, near Hythe, on the following day, both the work of a gang of men coming from Elham, Lyminge, and Stelling, villages which lay midway between Canterbury and Hythe. Altogether, at least 390 threshing machines were destroyed in the riots, the first in Kent but in larger numbers as the disturbances spread westwards and northwards in Wiltshire, Berkshire, Hampshire, and Norfolk.[23] Clearly the geographical distribution of the machine breaking depended in large part on the presence of the larger arable farms where the machines were in use; and large-scale arable farming was a feature especially of the Isle of Thanet in Kent, Salisbury Plain, the Norfolk sands, and the downlands of Berkshire and Hampshire.

The threshing machine, making its appearance near the end of the previous century, was first used in south-east Scotland and the north-east of England, where labour was scarcer and more expensive than in southern England. It seems to have spread rapidly during the labour shortages of the Napoleonic Wars, but was still in rather small numbers in southern counties in 1815. However, the use of the machine must then have grown considerably to explain the large numbers destroyed by the rioters in some southern counties – ninety-seven in Wiltshire alone.[24] It is perhaps remarkable that the machine spread at all in the south after 1815, given the cheapness of labour and the damage done to the straw by machine-threshing (the straw was much prized in some areas such as parts of Bedfordshire and Buckinghamshire where straw-plaiting was an important cottage industry). Further, it is clear that many larger farmers appreciated that any hands displaced by the machine were very likely to fall upon the parish, thus taking up in higher poor rates the value of labour savings made by the machine. On the other hand, the more rapid threshing made it possible for farmers to get their corn to market more quickly, enabling them to take advantage of prices that would be higher then than later in the autumn.

A puzzling aspect of the machine breaking was that, while some farmers did do their best to protect their machines, others merely stood by and let the destruction go on, even putting the machine out in the yard for the rioters to deal with, and sometimes encouraging the men with words, hammers, and beer. It is known that at least some of the more costly large machines, those worked by a large team of horses or by water-power, were insured, as were some farmers' houses, barns, and stacks. But it appears that many of the machines in use in the south at this time were small ones, driven by only a few horses or even by hand. Their cost was low; indeed, in 1829 a Mr Rider, 'a mechanic and small farmer' of Westbury in Wiltshire was reported to have invented a portable machine, the cost of which was unlikely to 'exceed £8 or £10'. It may well have been the appearance in the south of cheap machines of this sort that set off the labourers' trail of destruction, for machine-threshing was being put within the reach of every small producer of corn. Indeed, before the riots, the Mr Rider referred to was himself frightened by the labourers' hostility and 'acting on the advice of his friends, gave up making the machine . . . although other persons took up the trade'.[25]

The cheap machines were said to be too weak and inefficient to be satisfactory, and this may be one reason why the farmers were not always unhappy to have them broken up. Further, numbers of them were 'portable', carried round from farm to farm as required, and owned collectively by a group of farmers. Where the cost of the machine was spread in this way the loss to each individual farmer would be very small indeed. And again, it may well be that a farmer, hearing that a gang of machine breakers was coming his way, would be happy to sacrifice his machine if his house, barns, and stacks were left intact. Arson, indeed, was a far greater cause of loss than destruction of threshing machines. Although the more expensive water-powered machine cost about £500, the larger horse-driven models could be bought for about £100,[26] while damage by fire to farm buildings, livestock, and stacks could cost much more. A barn at Selling Court, near Faversham in east Kent, destroyed by fire on 24 October 1830, was valued at £1,000; and a farm at Borden, a few miles to the west, burned three days previously, at £1,500–2,000.[27]

Incendiarism and attacks on machinery were the most menacing expressions of the labourers' discontent. The symbols of their distress, the machines that took away winter employment, the barns and stacks that represented food they could not get, were not, however, at the root of their problems. This was lowness of wages, and the uncertain nature of employment threatened by machinery and the growth of numbers: in the thirty years after 1800 population had expanded by nearly 50 per cent in areas where there was little scope for more work on the land, where the geographical mobility of the labourers was limited, and where much of the old rural industry had disappeared or declined.

To some extent the violent face presented by elements of the revolt conceals the moderation of the men's demands. Especially in the first months, much of the rioting was perfectly open, the 'mob' made up of groups of neighbours or relations with leaders, often craftsmen, some of whose names have come down to us: John Adams, radical cobbler of Maidstone, 'Captain' Revell at Ash in east Kent, 'General' Moore of Garlinge who led machine breakers in the Isle of Thanet, Richard Knockolds in Norfolk, called 'Counsellor' by his followers, Thomas Hollis in Oxfordshire known as 'the King', and 'Captain' or 'Lord' Hunt, whose men struck at Fordingbridge in Hampshire and extended their operations to the neighbouring counties of Wiltshire and Dorset. Sometimes committees were formed, delegates coming from villages in the neighbourhood, and meetings were held to decide on the course of action. Itinerant bands marched from farm to farm, impressing recruits from field and cottage. Their leader wore a white hat or rode a white horse as a sign of authority, and his followers waved flags and blew on horns. Some carried formidable weapons and uttered ferocious language – 'blood for breakfast' and 'bread or blood' – but as the Attorney-General himself remarked, 'there has been such an absence of cruelty as to create general surprise'. Indeed, although some constables, overseers and parsons were manhandled and occasionally beaten up, not a single life was lost in the whole course of the riots among farmers, landlords, overseers, parsons, or the other objects of the labourer's anger.[28]

Some men believed that if the extent of their plight was brought to the notice of the more influential members of rural society, the large landowners and gentry, steps would be taken to put things right. On 29 October 1830 a crowd of about 300 gathered at East Sutton Park, near Maidstone, the home of Sir John Filmer. Their leader, John Adams, asked

Sir John if 'the Gentlemen would go hand in hand with the Labouring Classes to get the expenses of Government reduced'. After Sir John had given the men two sovereigns for 'refreshment' the crowd went away, only to reappear the same evening at the nearby house of the Rector of Langley. There they told the Rector's son that he must know the poor were starving, and that 'they were going round the country peacably to all the Gentlemen to procure their assistance in obtaining their rights'. Soon afterwards, on 2 November at Faversham in east Kent, a group of men, later swollen in numbers to 400, spoke of their intention of going round the farmers with a view to getting their wages raised to 2s. 6d. a day, and then to the landlords to make them lower their rents. 'They are very quiet', wrote an eyewitness, 'and all they require is more wages.'[29]

In the result the wages concessions gained in the heady days of 1830 were generally maintained, at least for a period, though this did not prevent the persistence of areas of extremely low wages, such as the 7s. a week that Caird found to be the 'common rate' on Salisbury Plain in 1850, with one large farmer paying only 6s.[30] Large parts of East Anglia and southern England were paying on average less than 9s. a week at that date, some less than 8s.: Swing achieved no revolution in farmworkers' pay. The destruction of threshing machines did cause a set-back in their use which lasted for some years, and as late as the 1860s farmers had to guard against deliberate damage to their growing array of machines. The threshing machine's return was usually in a new form: large mobile steam-driven machines, owned and operated by contractors who took them round from farm to farm.

Of more general significance was the effect of Swing on the course of reform. The agricultural rioting came to a peak when parliamentary reform was at a critical stage, and in Cobbett's view had more effect than the urban disturbances: 'I sowed the thoughts', he claimed vaingloriously, 'but it was the operations of poor Swing that made these thoughts spring up into action.'[31] And 'poor Swing' had also some influence in bringing in the New Poor Law of 1834 and Tithe Commutation in 1836 – both concerning matters that had incensed the labourers. And, in the long run, the movement for state-supported education drew strength from those who believed it to offer an answer to the labourers' poverty and naïvety.

The repression of Swing did not completely cow the southern labourer. Fires broke out again in the autumn of 1831 when the Lords rejected the second Reform Bill. There were isolated wages strikes with labourers having to be dispersed by the yeomanry, and the appearance of short-lived unions, including that of Tolpuddle. Some of the strikes, and riots too, were directed against the New Poor Law. And for twenty years after the first fires of 1830 burning barns and stacks lit up the night skies over East Anglia and large parts of southern England as men felt the urge to assert their grievances in a way that would frighten the propertied class while carrying little risk to themselves.[32] The killing and maiming of animals – ranging from stabbing and poisoning of horses to cutting off the ears of donkeys, the suffocating of sheep, and even more savage acts – was never so common as incendiarism, although Norfolk and Suffolk had between them over a hundred cases in the twenty years after Swing. It was however, like some of the fires, the result of personal feuds rather than an expression of social protest.[33]

Some 2,200 men were tried for offences committed during Swing: 800 were acquitted, 7 fined, 1 whipped, and 644 sent to jail. Of the remainder, 505 were sentenced to transportation and 252 to death; of the last, 19 were executed. It was a heavy retribution for riots in which no lives were lost by those attacked. Many villages were shorn of their young men, 'whole communities that, for a generation, were stricken by the blow'.[34]

Yet, as we have seen, the labourers were not entirely intimidated. For long years their grievances continued to fester, for the reform of Parliament, the Poor Law, and Tithes had done them little good. Their wages were still pitiful, their employment still precarious. Swing was not a revolution, nor had it achieved revolutionary benefits for the labourers. Southern farmworkers were still getting less than 12s. a week on average as late as 1870 – less than the men at Faversham had asked for on that day in early November 1830. They were still badly housed and fed, and little educated. A renewed attempt to better their lot, this time by the power of unionism, ran into the sands at the end of the 1870s. The farmworkers' answer was to leave the land, as thousands of country men and women had been doing in the decades since 1830. That year had failed to begin a process of amelioration that might have stemmed the exodus. Swing was a plea for men to have their rights, to maintain their title to a decent living. The laws of men, and of economics, denied such rights; and all the fires and smashing of machines had not been able to overcome the prior claims of property, the relentless grinding of the poor in the wheels of the market economy.

Notes

1 Hobsbawm and Rudé, 1973, appendix I.
2 Charlesworth, 1978, especially 37–9.
3 Hobsbawm and Rudé, 1973, 84, 201.
4 ibid., appendix I.
5 Caird, 1968, frontispiece, 512.
6 Cobbett, 1912, I, 248.
7 Hobsbawm and Rudé, 1973, 78–9, 91.
8 ibid., 57.
9 Cobbett, 1912, I, 266–7.
10 Hobsbawm and Rudé, 1973, 91–2, 122–3, 126–7.
11 Hammond and Hammond, 1978, 226.
12 Hobsbawm and Rudé, 1973, appendix III.

13   ibid., 182, 229; Spater, 1982, II, 475.
14   Spater, 1982, II, 474–7.
15   ibid., 474.
16   Hobsbawm and Rudé, 1973, 62, 72, 156.
17   ibid., 194–6.
18   ibid., 75, 123–4.
19   ibid., 219–20.
20   ibid., 97–8, 198; Hammond and Hammond, 1978, 192–3.
21   Hobsbawm and Rudé, 1973, appendix I.
22   ibid., 148–57.
23   ibid., appendices I, III.
24   Fox, 1978, 26–8.
25   ibid., 28.
26   Macdonald, 1975, 75; Macdonald, 1978, 31.
27   Hobsbawm and Rudé, 1973, 188–9.
28   ibid., 174–9.
29   ibid., 76–7.
30   Caird, 1968, 84.
31   Spater, 1982, II, 503.
32   Hobsbawm and Rudé, 1973, 243–5.
33   Archer, 1985, 147–57.
34   Hobsbawm and Rudé, 1973, 225.

4

Poachers abroad

John E. Archer

The polar forces of game preservation and poaching lie at the heart of eighteenth- and nineteenth-century rural society. All social classes from the wealthiest landlord down to the poorest labourer converged in the artificial landscape of coverts, walks, and closes, and there confronted one another in the most persistent, brutal, and bitter conflict the countryside experienced from the mid-eighteenth century onwards – the poaching war. The history of this war is codified in the game laws, a legal thicket of complex, anomalous, and prejudiced legislation which spilt 'the blood of men and boys'. No other set of laws was so consistently challenged and set at defiance, and they were perhaps the greatest source of conflict, not only in rural society, but in society as a whole after 1800. They lacked the consent of all but the governing classes, and even here the process of social and political change ensured that the urban middle class, too, came to despise them.

Historians have universally regarded the game laws as a classic example of class selfishness, and they have condemned their penalties as savage, though Munsche in his recent study has qualified this judgement by noting that the penalties for the theft of deer, hens, and rabbits were often far harsher.[1] Game, it should be emphasized, was narrowly defined to include hares, pheasants, partridges, and grouse, whereas deer, rabbits, and fish were covered by separate acts. However, the notorious Black Act of 1723, designed originally as a temporary bludgeon to strike at deer stealers, became a 'bloody code' for a hundred years, and was employed against night poachers who often went about their work disguised in wet soot or black gunpowder.

Birds like pheasant and partridge occupied a curious position in the legal history of this country, being neither private property nor *ferae naturae*. It was this rather uncertain perch which gave rise to two bitterly opposed views. On the one hand, the right to hunt game between 1671 and 1831 was restricted to an exclusive minority of 'qualified' gentry, who were defined as owners of land worth £100 a year, holders of ninety-nine year leases of land worth £150 a year, and the eldest sons of esquires, knights and nobles, and their gamekeepers. One often repeated remark is that the right to take game was fifty times more exclusive than the right to vote.[2] On the other hand, the poachers, supported by the unqualified community at large, made a strict moral distinction between theft and poaching. All the laws – and over forty Acts were passed before 1831 on matters concerning game – could not convince them against the idea that game was not only *ferae naturae* but also the property of those who took it. Justification for this stance was sought and found on the very first page of the Bible where God placed man 'in command of the fishes of the sea, and all that flies through the air'. One prison chaplain summarized the poacher's attitudes: 'game was made for the poor as well as the rich';[3] and the logic of this argument was stretched to include the murder of keepers through what poachers termed 'acts of self-defence'. Poaching was thus sanctioned and legitimized by the majority, which has led historians to regard it as the epitome of 'social crime'.[4]

Universal abhorrence among nearly all social classes may have placed game legislation in a rather paradoxical position, for as Cobbett maintained, 'It is nonsense to talk of peace and harmony in the country as long as that law should remain in existence.' And yet Hay, in his study of Cannock Chase, believes the game laws may have smoothed relations between masters and men which were strained at the best of times.[5] Neither the paradox nor the exclusivity of game disappeared with the 1831 reform, when the 'qualified' status was replaced by the game certificate. This provided the occupiers of land with the right to kill game provided they had first purchased a certificate. Theoretically, the gentry's monopoly had been broken, but a clause within the Act allowed landlords to retain sole hunting rights on their tenants' land if they so wished. This, in effect, rendered the reform meaningless since most landlords kept their shooting rights by altering their tenancy agreements.[6] Thus the exclusive privilege was jealously maintained into the Victorian age in spite of political attacks from John Bright and the Anti-Corn Law League, and later from the radicals who supported the cause of agricultural trade unionism.[7] Only near the end of the century was there some slight relaxation when the Ground Game Act of 1880 was passed. This allowed farmers 'the unalienable, concurrent right' to shoot hares and rabbits, whose numbers amounted to vermin proportions, on their land. However, the realities of rural authority and deference meant that many landlords were able to hold on to their sport. 'The Game Bill', said Disraeli, 'is a mere phantom.'[8]

The antithesis of the strict preserver was the poacher, who might be rural rebel, hungry labourer, angry farmer, or hard-nosed professional. All manner of country people of all classes and ages (although not sex, since poaching was predominantly a male pastime – women like Kit Nash of Hertfordshire who kept a ferret in a bag up her skirt and was eventually gaoled for shooting a policeman, were exceptional) came under this generic heading. Equally, a diversity of motives ranging from a love of sport to a love of money, a hungry belly to political hatred, urged men to transgress the law.

Strange though it may seem, identifying the poacher is for the historian a problem fraught with difficulties, especially before 1856: strange because in the first forty years of the nineteenth century poaching was the fastest growing crime. One-seventh of all criminal convictions in the 1840s were related to game, and even as late as 1870 there were over 10,000 game prosecutions. In 1843 a quarter of total male convictions in Berkshire, Hertfordshire, Oxfordshire, and Wiltshire were concerned with game, a third in Bedfordshire and Buckinghamshire, and two-fifths in Rutland.[9] The poacher's ubiquitousness meant that little was recorded or commented upon, for his presence was as regular as the shooting season. The manner in which he was tried and convicted and, likewise, the recording of his sentence, has led to obscurity and anonymity. The majority were summarily prosecuted for the least serious breaches of the game code, which until 1848 could be heard in the magistrate's home. Many therefore escaped the legal records, especially in the eighteenth century. Second, even in the following century, when documentation and statistics improved, the parliamentary papers covering criminal statistics failed to record any consistent long-term series of convictions until after 1856. Third, poachers could be, and were, prosecuted or disciplined in many other ways: dealt with privately, or under the Black Act, sacked from their jobs or evicted from their estate cottages. Last, and perhaps most important of all, only a very small minority were caught. The true extent of poaching was enormous.

The ever-increasing legislation on game over the two centuries, the growing intensity of preservation and its corollaries, effective slaughter and poaching, were inextricably linked and locked into a vicious spiral. This bloody momentum of dead game, murdered keepers, and maimed poachers reached its climax in the second quarter of the nineteenth century and became a part of the wider rural war then affecting much of southern and eastern England. However, it is the 'old game code' of 1671–1711 which established the ascendancy and privileges of the landed gentry, raising 'a little Nimrod in every manor'. In addition to the restrictive qualifications, the 1671 Act also proscribed the owning of hunting dogs, snares, nets, and other 'engines', property which could be seized by appointed gamekeepers. The penalty for an offence was fixed under the 1707 Act at £5 or three months imprisonment.[10] By the mid-eighteenth century, with developments in shooting and more systematic preservation, game came to assume a species of private property reserved for the privileged few. The desire to protect what was becoming an increasingly expensive hobby hardened. Professional keepers were widely introduced to rear pheasants and partridges and protect them from both vermin and poachers, though the two were often synonymous in the preserver's mind. The escalation in the costs – at Longleat for example, expenditure on pheasants rose from £264 in 1790 to £2,555 by 1856 – was in part a reflection of the changing fashion in hunting methods.[11] A healthy walk around the estate with dog and gun degenerated into a static ritualized slaughter by lined-up guns waiting for an army of beaters to bring them their bags. *Battue* shooting, as it was called, brought dramatic increases in the numbers of game bred and killed. A good day's shooting in Norfolk in 1790 accounted for 80 pheasants and 40 hares and partridges. Eighty years later Maharajah Duleep Singh, admittedly a fanatic, bagged 780 partridges by himself. One of the most obsessive preservers, the Prince of Wales, raised his annual tally of dead game at Sandringham from 7,000 a year to 30,000 in the late nineteenth century.[12]

With the dramatic increases in the game population, especially in the southern and eastern counties – amounting in the words of Hudson to 'the curse of the pheasant' – an equal and opposite reaction occurred.[13] The resident rural communities found temptation in every wood and hedgerow, a temptation made all the greater by the commercialization of poaching. In 1755 a total ban on the game trade was imposed which effectively gave poachers a complete monopoly of what eventually became a large and relatively open black market. They supplied publicans, higglers, and coachmen, who in turn sent their illicit wares to respectable poulterers at London's Leadenhall Market.[14] It was a profitable business since in the 1820s a poacher could hope to make 2s. from a hare and 3s. 6d. from a brace of pheasants. Thus a profitable night's hunting could easily outstrip the weekly wage of an agricultural labourer. This kind of arithmetic proved attractive to many, and even as early as 1787 William Marshall, writing of Norfolk, thought as many as 500 were principally dependent on poaching.

The gentry met this challenge in a number of ways, not least by establishing national and provincial associations to prosecute black marketeers and break up gangs which were fast becoming 'the terror of the countryside', though these bodies met with little success. Few poachers were willing to betray their fellows, although occasionally some turned king's evidence in order to escape transportation or worse. Hay found only eight cases of 'peaching' in over 200 incidents spread over half a century.[15] The most powerful weapon at the gentry's disposal was the law. As magistrates they combined the roles of judge and jury in summary convictions, and as legislators they were able to impose increasingly harsher laws, especially for night poaching. By 1800 two or more convicted of armed poaching were automatically imprisoned for six months with hard labour for a first offence. Subsequent offences could result in impressment into the armed forces, a very real threat at this time of European war. There soon followed the even more stringent Ellenborough Act of 1803, which imposed the death penalty on anyone resisting lawful arrest – in other words resisting keepers. Although the Napoleonic Wars brought some respite to preservers, since many poachers were away fighting, the peace of 1815 brought home more disciplined, ex-military men who offered even sterner resistance to the keepers. The gentry's reflex action was predictable: the Night Poaching Act of 1816, which imposed a mandatory penalty of seven years transportation; and although the Act was repealed and replaced the following year, armed poaching at night remained a transportable offence.

The stakes were now so high that most poaching gangs chose to stand their ground and fight when confronted by an army of keepers. 'There is hardly now a jail-delivery in which some gamekeeper has not murdered a poacher,' wrote Sydney Smith, 'or some poacher a gamekeeper.' Men were executed even though no murder had been committed, a fact graphically described by Hopkins in his powerful study. The real defect of these harsh laws was not their oppressiveness, Munsche concludes, but their ineffectualness.[16] They did nothing to stem the rising tide of poaching; the Night Poaching Acts were in fact self-defeating in their severity since juries were reluctant to find defendants guilty for what were regarded as relatively minor infractions of the law. Poachers were even acquitted by sympathetic juries where death to keepers had occurred during affrays. The 1817 Act, having defeated itself, was replaced by the slightly milder 1828 Act, which allowed imprisonment for first and second offenders and transportation for the more recalcitrant.

The defects of the Night Poaching Act had been highlighted by another development resorted to by desperate preservers – the deployment of mantraps and spring-guns. Predictably they made their first appearance in the 1770s in East Anglia, the nation's game larder, but they had become widespread by the turn of the century. These contraptions brought the danger of maiming and worse to both innocent and guilty wanderers of the woods, although as deterrents they were singularly unsuccessful. They maimed, shot, or killed all but their intended victims. Gamekeepers, old women out collecting wood, and even a botanically-minded curate fell victim to these indiscriminating guardians of the covers.[17] Admiral Wilson's three sons were all shot by a single charge from one of his own spring-guns, and poachers frequently made it a priority to discover the whereabouts of the hazards. They would trip them off or move them to new sites in order to hoist keepers by their own petards. By the 1820s 'the daily accidents and misfortunes', as Peel termed them, had become counter-productive even for many strict preservers, one of whom, Lord

Suffield, led the successful campaign to have them banned in 1827.[18] Evidence suggests that not all were removed, whilst other preservers resorted to 'wooden falsehoods' – signs warning trespassers that mantraps and spring-guns had been set in the woods.

Poaching, according to contemporary attitudes among magistrates and landowners, was 'the root of all evil'. The game laws, after all, had been enacted to prevent 'persons of inferior rank' from squandering their time. The poor not only needed the discipline of work but also protection from their own intimate propensity to be immoral. The Duke of Grafton spoke for many when he contended that poaching gave rise to idleness, drunkenness, and a disinclination to work by virtue of the poacher's turning night into day and spending his time and money in the beer dens. The Hon. Grantly Fitzhardinge Berkeley was more forthright: the poacher's objects, in his opinion, were beer, gambling, riot, and debauchery.[19] So emerged a stereotype of a wan-faced idler and criminal well on the road to the gallows. The poacher further compounded his poor reputation by not only bagging his game at night when it was most vulnerable, but also by devaluing its status by sale. The poacher, to put it bluntly, was not only in trade but also unsporting.

In reality poachers were more prosaic characters and their identities as diverse as their motives. Historians have frequently attempted to differentiate them, the professional from the casual, the gang member from the wily loner, but inevitably an overlap between the different groups occurs.[20] As 99 per cent of the population were not allowed to hunt, it seems reasonable to attempt some kind of categorization, while acknowledging the drawbacks of such an exercise. One group more common than the legal records suggest can be best termed 'gentleman sportsmen', to coin a contemporary euphemism which covered two groups of uninvited hunters. First, before 1831 there were the 'qualified' like Captain Hawker of the 14th Light Dragoons, who shot when and where he pleased – sometimes from the top of a mail coach – until warned off by the keepers.[21] The second and much larger group included all manner of middling classes: poaching parsons, Eton schoolboys, solicitors, surgeons, and police inspectors but, above all, tenant-farmers. 'Men who are quite respectable', observed the chaplain of Appleby gaol, 'will snare a hare, or go out with a gun.'[22] Their absence from the court records highlights one of the galling facts of the game laws, that prosecutors had considerable discretionary power at their disposal. In effect, the better-off settled the matter out of court, or in the case of Berkeley, a noted pugilist, by a bout of fisticuffs, whereas labourers faced a series of cumulative penalties if the prosecutor so chose. Farmers suffered the game laws with particular bitterness, partly because their social pretensions had risen during the Napoleonic Wars, but more importantly because game frequently devastated their root and corn crops. This problem became the focus of the 1846 Select Committee which heard evidence on the startlingly large amount of damage perpetrated by hare and winged game. A Mr Chambers of Beechamwell, Norfolk, suffered £1,000 worth of damage, and farms on the Elvedon estate were left untenanted.[23] Faced with ruin some farmers took matters into their own hands and initiated culls for which they were evicted.

Poaching was a skilled craft requiring years of experience, and most practitioners served their apprenticeship as bored crow scarers. Time, observation, and inquisitiveness were facets which children possessed in abundance. Many professionals recalled their first bag: James Hawker, a radical cobbler, started as a 14-year-old, while the anonymous self-styled 'King of the Norfolk poachers' trapped his first hare at 9 and was in Norwich gaol by the time he was 12.[24] In one skill – egg stealing – children excelled over adults, and through this they were introduced to the local professionals and the black market. Poaching, therefore, was built into their agricultural work experience.

The dividing line between the casual opportunist and the professional was often blurred, though the extremes were clear. Considerable indirect evidence suggests that most poached for the pot. The rise in poaching convictions coincided, temporally and geographically, with increased preservation, *battue* shooting, and a declining standard of living in arable regions. The tempting presence of a vast profusion of semi-tame birds proved too much for the half-starved workforce who, in the words of the Hammonds, poached in order to 'rehabilitate their economic plight'.[25] The major peak in indictments, (1828, 1843, and 1849) suggest, as Hobsbawm and Rudé have argued, that poaching can be used as an index of rising social tensions in the village.[26] On all three occasions riots or incidents of arson followed soon after. Poaching was not only an act of hunger, it was also an act of defiance. Further evidence presented by Howkins on Oxfordshire confirms the casual nature and poverty-based aspect of crime. He discovered that 75 per cent of those arrested had travelled no more than two miles to catch their quarry (while professionals travelled up to thirty miles), and most were caught in the winter months. Seasonal poaching thus coincided with seasonal unemployment and food shortages, and should be regarded in the same light as other scavenging crimes like the theft of wood and berry picking.[27]

Many of these casual poachers were described as 'capital workmen' or 'very respectable' by their employers. One young Suffolk labourer, Robert Collins, with no previous convictions and an excellent character reference, committed suicide when he was caught. Even the police admitted that many of the prosecuted were, in normal circumstances, completely law-abiding. The equally realistic Lord Suffield put the matter bluntly when addressing that citadel of game preservation, the House of Lords:

The recipe to make a poacher will be found to contain a very few and simple ingredients . . . Search out (and need not go far) a poor man, single, having his natural sense of right and wrong . . . give him little more than a natural disinclination to go to work, let him exist in the midst of lands where the game is preserved, keep him cool in winter, by allowing him insufficient wages to purchase fuel; let him feel hungry upon the small pittance of parish relief; and if he be not a poacher; it will be only by the blessing of God.[28]

Little wonder, as Joseph Arch recalled, that 'every other man you met was a poacher'.[29]

The distinction between casual and professional can be difficult to draw in years of agrarian distress. Temporarily laid-off young men took up poaching to provide themselves with alternative income. Frederick Gowing, Suffolk's most notorious poacher, gave the 1846 Select Committee an authentic account of the operation and of the uncertain distinction between part-timers and full-timers. Unemployed labourers, he explained, preferred the risk of imprisonment to incarceration in the workhouse because 'in goal they cannot hear the cries and screams of their children, nor the complaints of their wives, that is what vexes them'. After harvest Gowing reckoned on finding a hundred men in ten or fifteen villages who were willing to work for him. Once on his payroll they had to observe his rules; not to go armed with bludgeons, and only to work in small parties. He lent out snares, nets, and air guns, and bought their catches.[30]

Gowing's unusually non-violent organization was in direct contrast to the notorious and violent gangs which mushroomed in East Anglia after 1800.[31] Often drawn from the same social milieu, though slightly younger, they displayed a recklessness not commonly associated with country people. This was not altogether surprising since a full-time professional depended for his living on staying free of unnecessary trouble, whereas the young unemployed were often the most desperate and vengeful. They had little to lose. Other groups mixed their legitimate seasonal occupations with winter poaching. Herring fishermen on the east coast, for example, used nets of a different kind once the fishing was over. Another longstanding group, the 'Westleton gang', were sheep-dippers, fishermen, or poachers depending on the time of year.[32]

Full-time professionals were generally of a different order, though they, too, could encompass many different types of individual. The gangs were highly organized with many sub-cultural trappings, inhabiting a world of brothels and receivers. One of the most infamous in Suffolk was the thirty-strong 'Ixworth gang' who set up their headquarters at the Chequers Inn in Thetford. They possessed a treasurer, an armourer, a bank account, and good transport facilities, and were eventually broken up by a 'game spy' who infiltrated them.[33] The true professionals preferred to work alone, or at most with one or two 'pals' and a well-trained lurcher dog. Another, 'King of the Norfolk poachers', George Burton, unusually preferred the company of his wife. Many paid out large sums in fines over the course of their careers. Both Burton of Swaffham and Gowing had paid out over £200 apiece, and the latter had even employed a solicitor until the latter himself was poached by the preservers.[34] These men had the closest links with receivers and with carriers like stagecoach drivers and railwaymen – the latter would stop their trains to pick up game hampers.[35] Most of the live game and eggs were stolen from East Anglia, and most of the customers, keepers, and preservers came also from the same region. One of the scandals of preservation was that preservers were party to the commercialism of poaching.

The keepers were often drawn into the shadowy world of professional poaching in order to assuage the voracious hunting instincts of their employers, whose social standing by the mid-nineteenth century was measured by the size of the slaughter of each day's shoot. Needless to say, zealous keepers drove birds from neighbouring covers, bought eggs and store birds, and sold dead game to make up their salaries, sometimes with tragic consequences. Two of Lord Stradbroke's men committed suicide because they had been involved in illicit dealings with poachers and as a consequence had left the estate denuded of game.[36]

One feature, overlooked by many rural historians, is the fact that many poachers were neither agricultural labourers nor village dwellers. Counties like Lancashire, Staffordshire, and Yorkshire had their fair share of poachers who emanated from industrial towns. The coming of the railway brought a new mobility to relatively well-paid and fully-employed miners, weavers, Sheffield cutlers, and Reading 'Biscuit Boys'.[37] To them poaching was neither a business nor a necessity, except in times of dire distress. The Cotton Famine of the 1860s, for example, brought many weavers from the silent mills to the countryside. At Blackburn the trial of eight poaching weavers touched off a riot in which the town hall, police station, and court were stoned.[38] The motivation behind much urban poaching was in part a mixture of weekend sport and class hatred. Lacking the deference of their country counterparts, and possessing a trade union solidarity, the industrial gangs were perhaps the most formidable of them all. Moving in groups of seventy and eighty strong, many of them armed, they stripped the countryside and did not hesitate to wound or kill keepers who chanced upon them. It is more likely that the thrill of the fight was equal to the sport. Even in traditional rural counties like Norfolk many of the more brazen gangs worked out of towns such as Norwich and Great Yarmouth. One of these gangs, known as the 'North Sea Pirates', sailed along the Broads plundering and poaching the grounds adjoining the banks.[39]

While deer, rabbits, and salmon were legally not game, rural communities made little or no distinction between them and the legal variety. Their determination to retain their rights to such creatures led to violent rural wars, more protracted and intense than anything witnessed nightly in the game covers. Two episodes from the eighteenth century concerning the Windsor Blacks and Cannock Chase, have been fully documented, and in both cases the commoners' struggle escalated into anonymous acts of arson and animal maiming.[40] Nothing comparable occurred in the nineteenth century, although poachers continued to find themselves at the head of battles over fishing rights or rabbits on newly-enclosed land. The fishing war, which entered the scene relatively late, reached frightening proportions in the 1860s and 1880s in Devon, the Lake District, Radnorshire, and Breconshire. David Jones, in his study of the Welsh struggle, noted the strong element of community ritual and organization in which men dressed themselves as 'Rebecca', a self-conscious echo of the earlier 1843 riots.[41] In counties where salmon and trout were absent the sense of grievance frequently centred on the rabbit. One ten-year-long dispute at Holt, Norfolk, brought a poacher to national prominence as the 'village Hampden . . . the defender of the people's rights to the people's rabbits'.[42] Men like Doughty were natural community leaders, independent, intelligent, fearless, and in the words of another radical poacher, James Hawker, prepared to take on 'the Class'.[43] They belonged to a distinguished tradition of radical poachers, acting as tribunes and the vanguard of the farm labourers in their struggles over work, wages, and poor relief.

The relationship between poaching and other rural crimes is a complex one and contemporary opinion was often divided on the subject. Few strict preservers would have disagreed with the 1846 Select Committee's conclusion that poaching was 'the first stage in the career of a rural criminal'. The belief had acquired by then the status of natural law: 'poachers', said a Surrey Magistrate, 'are all poultry stealers, and sheep stealers also – they acquire the disposition of a savage or a wild beast – a disposition which must lead to robbery and every species of nocturnal depredation.'[44] Occasionally such assertions were supported with evidence. Gloucestershire's chief constable said of 110 poachers in his county that as many as 91 had committed larceny, sheep stealing, burglary, highway robbery, and housebreaking.[45] Moreover, many acts of murder and grievous bodily harm in the countryside were the result of violent affrays. Contrasting with this opinion was the adamant assertion of many professional poachers who claimed that 'a poacher is not a thief and a thief is not a poacher'. Some gentry were forced to concur. One wrote:

I may say safely, that poaching is a great source of evil, though it is an extraordinary fact that many practise the offence without committing more serious breaches of the law. There are in this district, annual, biennial, and triennial visitants to the gaol for poaching . . . some of whom have been as many as a dozen times for offences against the Game Laws, yet never convicted of felony.[46]

Both opinions contain an element of truth. Certainly the forces which brought the young unemployed together to form temporary and violent gangs would have inclined them towards the stealing of fowls and sheep. But for the genuinely addicted there was probably little other involvement since the practicalities of poaching were different from those of other forms of theft. Game was easier to steal and it usually carried a lesser sentence.

Poachers, too, were thought to share an affinity with arsonists. Both planned and drank in the same alehouse, it was argued, and both attacked property owners under the cover of darkness. This relationship was thought to be particularly pronounced in the 1840s when East Anglia was ablaze with incendiary fires. Particular villages, Hadleigh, Polstead, and Stanton in Suffolk, to name but three, were notorious as centres of poaching and incendiarism where arsonists furthered vendettas which had arisen out of game disputes. George Head, sentenced to gaol for poaching, announced 'he would not go in for nothing. We are going to coop tomorrow, but we'll have a damned good flare up before we go.' In another case a barn was fired because a hunting dog had been destroyed. As Jones has written, poachers 'waged social war in every way they knew'.[47]

With the introduction of rural constabularies between 1839 and 1856 one would have expected the police to join the keepers in the front line of the poaching war. Some chief constables, however, showed a marked reluctance to become involved in what they regarded as a private battle in which they could run the risk of being identified as keepers under a different guise and, moreover, ones paid for out of public money. Gaining the public's trust and respect, not the gentry's thanks, was generally uppermost in their minds, though this changed with the 1862 Poaching Prevention Act which authorized the police to harass the labouring community. They now had the power to stop and search 'any person whom they may have good cause to suspect of coming from any land where he shall have been unlawfully in search or pursuit of Game'. The passing of this law, said Joseph Arch, was 'a black day for the labourer . . . T'was as if so many Jacks-in-the-Box had been set free to spring out on the labourer from hedge or ditch.'[48]

The police were fortunate in so far as they entered the 'long affray' only in the second half of the nineteenth century. Until then, and for many decades to come, it was the gamekeepers who bore the greatest injury and hatred from the community at large. Generally disowned and forced to live alone among their charges, keepers gave themselves 'airs' and were always 'sneaking about' watching labourers and farmers at their work. As agents of game preservers the law gave them considerable powers, a fact reflected in the harsher penalties imposed on those who assaulted them as distinct from assaults on the police. They could search homes without a warrant, confiscate 'engines', and kill cats and dogs, measures they carried out with relish: one Dorset keeper destroyed 300 cats in a year. However, it was their attitude to dogs which gave rise to most hostility. Not only lurchers, the linchpin of the gang, but farm dogs, too, were shot, and in some cases ritually hanged in mock-Tyburn style.[49]

The number of keepers expanded rapidly from the late eighteenth century and continued rising to the end of the nineteenth, by which time they far outnumbered the rural constabularies. Armies of keepers and watchers guarded the covers. At Gunton in Norfolk, for example, there were six full-time keepers and seventy watchers, of whom eight were on duty every night of the season.[50] Confronting them were battalions of poachers, disguised, armed, and determined to resist arrest. The poaching war raged for decades after 1815, and local newspapers carried weekly reports of 'desperate' and 'dreadful' affrays. At Methwold in Norfolk the watch called out squire Jones, who on hearing a gun go off in his plantation, cried out 'My men, what are you doing there?' The reply came back on the night air: 'you b. . . . r we come for pheasants, and pheasants we'll have.'[51] This typical encounter left one watcher dead and others severely wounded. More audacious gangs, their confidence reinforced by strength of numbers, would pay keepers a visit before setting about their night's work. They barricaded them in their cottages or shot in through their windows, and in some cases took the keepers prisoner and, on pain of death, walked them around the covers.[52] In terms of casualties the keepers lost this war. In the fifteen years between 1833 and 1848 as many as forty-six were killed, and in 1844, a typical year, thirty-one were seriously wounded and two murdered.[53] While the violence gradually subsided in the southern regions after the mid-century, the northern counties, close to the moors, became the scenes of extremely violent confrontations.

Only by the end of the century, with improved policing, shifts in morality, changing economic circumstances, and social improvements, had poaching showed marked decline. It was by then, wrote Flora Thompson, regarded as 'a mug's game'.[54] Leisure and necessity no longer stood confronting one another in the game preserves, and the war of attrition had been won by neither side. It had simply become an anachronism.

Notes

1 Munsche, 1981a, 159–60; Hammond and Hammond, 1920, 162–75.
2 Hay *et al.*, 1975, 189; Munsche, 1981a, 8–27.
3 Book of Genesis, verses 20–6; BPP 1846, IX, pt 2, xxxvii.
4 Rule, 1979, 135–53.
5 Hopkins, 1985, 154; Hay *et al.*, 1975, 212.

6   Hopkins, 1985, 199.
7   Kirby, 1932, 18–37.
8   Hopkins, 1985, 268–9.
9   Horn, 1980, 178–9; Jones, 1982, 62.
10 Munsche, 1981a, 21.
11 Horn, 1980, 172.
12 Johnson, 1981, 13; Chenevix-Trench, 1967, 172; Munsche, 1981a, 37.
13 Hudson, 1911, 303.
14 Munsche, 1981a, 104; Hay *et al.*, 1975, 203.
15 Hay *et al.*, 1975, 199.
16 Horn, 1980, 177; Munsche, 1981a, 104.
17 Michael J. Carter, 1980, 16–17; Hopkins, 1985, 166–7; *Bury and Norwich Post*, 27 October 1824, 24 May 1826.
18 Hammond and Hammond, 1920, 171; Hopkins, 1985, 173.
19 Chenevix-Trench, 1967, 156.
20 Jones, 1979, 841–2; Porter, 1982, 97; Hopkins, 1985, 24–5.
21 Chenevix-Trench, 1967, 148–9.
22 Jones, 1982, 75; Hawker, 1978, 104; Munsche, 1981a, 52.
23 BPP 1846, IX, pt 1, 413–44; BPP 1873, XIII, 314.
24 Hawker, 1978, 4; Rider Haggard, 1974, 32.
25 Hammond and Hammond, 1920, 162.
26 Hobsbawm and Rudé, 1973, 57, 245.
27 Howkins, 1979, 279–82.
28 Michael J. Carter, 1980, 9–10.
29 Arch, 1986, 13.
30 BPP 1846 IX, pt 1, 629–34.
31 Michael J. Carter, 1980, *passim*.
32 BPP 1846, IX, pt 1, 312.
33 *Bury and Norwich Post*, 4 February, 24 March, 31 March 1852.
34 Glyde, 1894, 49.
35 Chenevix-Trench, 1967, 166.
36 Hopkins, 1985, 201–2; *Bury and Norwich Post*, 3 July 1844.
37 Chevenix-Trench, 1967, 166; Hopkins, 1985, 203.
38 ibid., 238.
39 Archer, 1982b, 374–5.
40 E.P. Thompson, 1975; Hay *et al.*, 1975, 189–253.
41 Porter, 1982, 96–107; Jones, 1976b, *passim*.
42 Archer, 1982b, 400–3.
43 Hawker, 1978, 95.
44 Munsche, 1981a, 54; BPP 1846, IX, pt 2, 251.
45 BPP 1846, IX, pt 2, xxxii.
46 Glyde, 1856b, 155.
47 Jones, 1982; Archer, 1982b, 393.
48 Hopkins, 1985, 239.
49 Munsche, 1981a, 82–3; Hopkins, 1985, 43; Hay *et al.*, 1975, 196; Munsche, 1981b, 82–105.
50 Archer, 1982b, 357.
51 Michael J. Carter, 1980, 29–31.
52 Archer, 1982b, 358.
53 Horn, 1980, 179.
54 Flora Thompson, 1973, 154.

5

Under cover of night: arson and animal maiming

John E. Archer

In his Christian allegorical history of the 'English peasant', Richard Heath
wrote of the labourers 'descending into Hell' in the years between 1815
and 1850:[1] a particularly apt metaphor, for the pages of provincial
newspapers from that period are filled with reports of 'diabolical outrages',
'devilish deeds', and 'demonic spirits'. Incendiarism, 'a hell above ground'
as one arsonist described his work, was promoted through the invention
of the 'lucifer' or strike-anywhere match in 1829–30. The lucifer, because
of its effectiveness, portability, and cheapness, liberated would-be pro-
testers at a moment when oppression, hatred, and poverty were most
keenly felt. In the years leading up to the mid-century, arguably the worst
two decades of the century for rural labourers, rural terrorism became the
active response to the defeat of Swing. One senses a new spirit of anger
and viciousness; crime in all its guises increased, but most notably the
protest crimes of arson, animal maiming, the sending of threatening letters, and physical attacks on farmers, poor law officials, and, later, the
police. Much of these were covert, under cover of darkness, and usually
the work of one or two individuals. It would be erroneous, however, to
explain away these acts as private feuds or vendettas since such guerilla
attacks left counties 'grinning with new fires' in which the burning stacks
became focal points of communal elaboration.

Recent historical debate has centred on whether covert protest was new
or traditional.[2] Arson and animal maiming had undoubtedly existed for
centuries; it had been legislated against under the Black Act of 1723, and
then not for the first time. As far back as 1545 the 'devilish act' of cutting
out the tongues of horses and cattle was sufficiently common for a statute
to be enacted.[3] However, the late eighteenth and early nineteenth centuries witnessed the gradual growth of rural protest crime: 1816, for example,
was described by one Victorian observer as the first year of incendiarism.

Furthermore, a dormant clause of the Black Act, which allowed victims of incendiary fires to claim compensation from their hundreds, was only resurrected in the years after 1815. Subsequently, in 1827, the government saw fit to remove this clause from the statute book, when, it must be assumed, the law had become a liability to rate-payers.[4] After 1830, until at least 1852, the scale and intensity of arson marked it out as being the hallmark of rural protest. Endemic protest crimes should not therefore be viewed as 'traditional' or 'pre-industrial' responses. They were individual acts of men who had learnt to their cost in 1830 that rural society was no longer paternal and traditional but capitalist, uncaring, and subject to the forces of the market economy. Arson, to echo Hobsbawm and Rudé, represented the labourers' failure 'to constitute themselves a class and to fight collectively as such' – a point emphasized through the sheer numbers of fires which broke out with alarming frequency immediately after the suppression of the 1830 riots, and again after the implementation of the New Poor Law in the southern and eastern counties in 1835–6.[5]

Many factors conspired to reduce labourers to demoralized pauperdom. The workforce of rural England continued to expand until 1851, after which migration, emigration, and new employment opportunities in the police and army and on the railways brought about a lessening of competition for agricultural work. Inevitably, population growth in the 1840s built up pressure for housing and work, and in some areas wages fell to miserable levels between 1849 and 1881. Furthermore, agriculture stagnated in the long-running post–1815 depression, with wheat prices, which in arable areas largely determined wage rates, never attaining the levels of the Napoleonic war boom. Prices fluctuated between 70s. a quarter during a brief spell of prosperity in the late 1830s and the low point of 38s.6d. reached during the mid-century depression. The other important factor which dominated the labourers' limited horizons was the implementation of the New Poor Law after 1834, which brought in its wake a further round of riots and disturbances to Cornwall, Devon, Kent, Sussex, and much of East Anglia. The stringency of this new act, for example in its workhouse test and, indeed, the very existence of the new-style workhouse itself, has perhaps been overstated in the past; but the reformed poor law did create justifiable fears among labouring communities, and introduced new practices which led to a further deterioration of living standards. The deterioration was felt particularly by the young single men finding themselves laid off in greater numbers by rates-conscious employers who found it cheaper to employ married family men with their wives and children.

The condition and attitudes of the rural labourers of this period are well known; numerous contemporaries took it upon themselves to discover the 'true state of rural England', and the reports they placed before their readers revealed a situation nothing short of scandalous. *The Times* sent Thomas Campbell Foster, the finest investigative reporter of his age; the *Morning Chronicle* on more than two occasions sent reporters on tour; and virtually every journal of note from *Punch* to *Fraser's Magazine* expressed strong views on the subject. In addition, concerned and knowledgeable individuals, Godolphin Osborne in the West Country, and in the east the Rev. J. S. Henslow, the first professor of botany at Cambridge, wrote informed and sensitive pamphlets and letters. These commentators may have disagreed on particulars but all were unanimous that 'the labourer has nothing to lose, nothing to defend, and nothing to hope for'.[6] What they found was a mass of barely literate men: of the 245 charged with arson in 1844 only 11 per cent were able to read and write well, and from Suffolk Glyde reported that a third of the parishes were without a school.[7] Moreover, the New Poor Law indirectly forced parents to cut short what little education there was for their children by sending them out to work at as early an age as possible. In such circumstances social mobility out of their class or occupation was virtually impossible. A visiting American journalist observed: 'they remain a distinct and servile class without any power of rising above their condition'. By the 1840s the labourer had become 'grave, moody and silent', seldom looking the farmer in the face. He was a 'discontented man, and, in sober earnest . . . he has good cause to be so'.[8]

The causes were indeed numerous, and they are almost impossible to generalize about. As E.P. Thompson observed, it is impossible to find an 'average' labourer.[9] The uneven process of proletarianization wrought changes in employment and working relations at different times in different parts of the country. The tradition of living-in, for example, had all but disappeared from East Anglia by 1830 although it was still a feature in the north in the 1870s. Annual hirings, which still occurred in the north, had died out in much of southern and eastern England, where it became common practice to employ unskilled labourers – who did not work with animals – by the day. Wages not only varied from the arable east to the pasture west and from north to south of the Wash, but even varied by as much as 2s. a week in a single village. All accounts acknowledge that there were pockets of appallingly low wages: 6s. a week (if there were no layoffs for wet weather) was reported from south-west Suffolk, while in Wiltshire the miserable 5s. drove labourers to meet openly and advertise their plight. A. L. Bowley's survey of wages shows conclusively how low wages had sunk throughout central and southern England by 1850.[10] It is worth pointing out in this context that a farm labourer could earn more in one night fighting an incendiary fire than he could in a week on the farm, a fact not lost on John Stallan, a Cambridgeshire pyromaniac, who received 6s.6d. for each of the twelve fires he started.[11]

More important even than low wages in any study of protest crime is the question of unemployment and under-employment. In years of incendiarism came reports of men 'lolling upon ditch-sides' or 'idly congregating on village greens', speaking 'bitterly of the farmers who would not give them work'. At Rattle Row, Norfolk, Foster fell into conversation with John Sturman, a 35-year-old father of four, who told him that in June he had had only five and a half days work and as a result had been forced to pull up half ripe potatoes from his garden.[12] Seasonal unemployment was a feature of the arable farming cycle when long lay-offs during the winter months was the normal experience for the casually employed. This was compounded by the return of the threshing machines, particularly to the eastern counties. The weather, too, could produce unexpected problems, as in the case of the drought of 1844 when hoeing was suspended because weeds had simply failed to grow.

The 'rural war' predicted by William Cobbett as a result of the New Poor Law, was temporarily postponed in the late 1830s during a brief spell of agrarian prosperity. However, from 1843 it was put under its severest test, and in Foster's opinion it was the single most important contributory cause of incendiarism. With such partisan views, Foster had little difficulty in finding labourers expressing hatred for the union workhouse and the guardians: 'Unless something be absolutely done about these unions, the fires will go on,' one warned, and another commented: 'the union distresses people and drives them mad.' What his highly partial accounts did bring to light was an illegal abuse called the 'ticket system', which according to Digby existed in six eastern counties.[13] Whether this system was the cause of so many fires, as Foster attempted to prove, is questionable. It is more than likely that it contributed further to the labourer's general antagonism towards the poor law. Of more significance was the guardians' reluctance to offer outdoor relief to unmarried labourers who in times of depression were offered the workhouse or nothing. The majority chose the latter and lived off their native wit, which in effect meant turning to crime, since the other safety nets of charity and allotments were also withheld from them.

Set against this background of poverty and insecurity, the living conditions of many were dire. Housing was cramped, disease-ridden, and basic. Osborne thought Dorset cottages were nothing but 'slightly improved hovels', while *The Times* described the eastern counties' mud huts with papered-up windows. Food was plain and dull and, ironically, inadequate. 'We work hard' one labourer complained, 'we till and sow the land till there is an abundance of food, and our reward is starvation.' During a spate of plough-breaking at Charlton-on-Otmoor in Oxfordshire a pathetic note was left: 'A full belly does not know what empty one feels.'[14] Bread and potatoes formed the staple diet and tea the principal beverage, which in 1844 was often brewed from peppermint or burnt crusts of toast. Meat was a rare treat, usually reserved for the head of the household, but cheese was common, though its quality left a lot to be desired. Suffolk cheese, known as 'bang' was so hard 'dogs bark at it because they could not bite it'.

Incendiarism was the most significant response to oppression, and as a weapon of intimidation, vengeance, bargaining, or terror it had many advantages. It was a quick, easy, cheap, and effective form of protest which could be carried out with relative impunity. Although more research on the subject is required, it is possible from the commitment figures to identify years when arson reached epidemic proportions. Before 1830 committals never rose above 47 a year in England and Wales, but immediately following the Swing Riots they rose sharply to over 100 a year in 1831–2, levelling out between 1833 and 1836, and then falling between 1837 and 1841. The 1840s experienced two enormous peaks, 245 in 1844 and 220 in 1849. In all, over 1,500 stood trial for arson between 1842 and 1851. A long-term decline set in after 1852, but further peaks occurred in 1862–4 and 1868–9.[15] Interestingly, the advent of agricultural trade unionism did not lead to the extinction of this crime, and reports of its being employed in trade disputes can be found up to the First World War.

Arson was not only the weathercock of rural protest, it was also remarkably persistent. Whilst annual committals can serve only as a guide to the actual scale of the crime – in East Anglia, for example, one person was convicted for every seven fires which occurred in the 1840s – they do indicate a pattern. Arson tended to coincide with low wheat prices, and hence low wages and high unemployment. The regional pattern, however, is more interesting since it was geographically more widespread than Swing. It was endemic in East Anglia, where the counties of Cambridgeshire, Essex, Norfolk, and Suffolk accounted for nearly 50 per cent of the 1844 indictments. But even within this area regional variations are apparent with Cambridgeshire and Huntingdon experiencing far greater incendiary activity after 1844, and especially between 1849 and 1851 when Caird reported farmers living 'in constant apprehension'.[16] Other counties, Bedfordshire, Berkshire, Devon, and Yorkshire, figure prominently in these later years but, surprisingly, former Swing counties like Kent and Sussex were less affected than they had been in the 1830s.

The bare statistics cannot even begin to convey the damage and fear caused by these 'flare-ups'. Many were not minor stack fires. Often working between Friday and Sunday, incendiaries frequently chose windy evenings thus ensuring maximum fire spread. At Bagshot, Surrey, two separate fires on Prince Albert's plantation converged and 'the flames at one time extended two miles in length and upwards of a mile in breadth'. This picture of a charred and smouldering landscape was repeated in Cambridgeshire, where it was reported that over ten square miles, 'no homestead remains'. In whatever county one looks massive damage was reported: thirty cottages at Winsham, Somerset, where a fire had been kindled during divine service, a popular time for vengeance to strike: or Dunstable, Bedfordshire, where the Wesleyan Chapel, together with sixty-four other buildings, were consumed.[17] The Cambridgeshire villages of Cottenham, Fordham, and Soham, which experienced between twelve and fifteen fires apiece, were burnt and rebuilt and burnt again in the late 1840s. The Norwich Union Insurance Company was forced in the end to refuse insurance to farmers in this county, and also those in Bedfordshire and Hertfordshire in 1850.[18]

Alarm and apprehension were greatest in the years 1843–4, 'when the incendiary stalked the length and breadth of the country'. A cursory study of newspaper reports places the number of attacks in excess of 600, with Norfolk and Suffolk accounting for 300 of them. In the former county fear of the flames spread even to the labouring communities, who listened 'with utmost consternation' to two enterprising preachers predicting the end of the world through 'universal conflagration'.[19] Not only were stacks and farms set alight but parsonages, inns, workhouses, and heathlands were destroyed. Primitive fire-fighting equipment was set aside and sub-scriptions raised to purchase fire engines, manufactured by none other than Ransomes, the makers of the threshing machines frequently singled out for destruction by the incendiaries.

The fires reached their zenith in December 1843, but what made this outbreak unique was that they continued unabated until the harvest of 1844, a fact which caused bewilderment to contemporaries. 'The supposed motives too have ceased to exist . . . the scenes of December and January re-enacted in May, a time of year when field labour is abundant.'[20] As a result, farmers came up with some bizarre theories which local labourers did much to promote. Strangers, invariably well dressed, were sighted in the vicinity of fires, many of whom were thought to be members of the Anti-Corn Law League or 'foreign agents' bent on promoting imported wheat. Oddly enough, one convicted arsonist, James Lankester, did argue that fires would raise wheat prices and hence wages.[21] Tramps, too, came under immediate suspicion and were rounded up. 'Many of the fires', Sir James Graham, the Home Secretary, told the House of Commons, 'were the act of one and the same incendiary . . . probably perambulating the district in question'.[22] When one considers that 600 fires occurred at this time the 'perambulating' incendiary was clearly an energetic figure. Graham could have given this risible theory greater credibility had he mentioned Leech Borley, one of Suffolk's most extraordinary arsonists. Borley's claim to fame, apart from his poaching, animal maiming, and incendiary activities, was his running ability. An oversight of the police, forgetting to remove his specially made running shoes after his arrest, had amusing consequences. Having been found guilty and sentenced to Van

Dieman's Land, Borley jumped from the dock and ran out of the court across Bury market-place to freedom.[23]

The majority of farmers and landowners simply refused to believe that their 'kind, simple, honest-hearted' men could do the work of demons, although evidence from 1844 and other years before 1852 indicates that most incendiaries lit fires in their own villages. For this reason arson was the most accurate gauge for measuring the state of social relations between employers and employees. This is backed up by the press reports which condemned the 'reckless indifference' and 'evident lukewarmedness' of spectators at the scene of conflagrations. Upwards of a thousand attended such sights and in the light of the dancing flames 'jeered and laughed at the men who worked the engines'. On other occasions spectators took wood with them to stoke up the flames, cut hose pipes, stoned firemen, and even refused money if they would help. Looting too, was not unusual: at Greenstead Hall, Essex, 'many attended for the sole purpose of plunder, for a body of them smashed the windows of the house, and nearly gutted it'. Those who had discovered the wine cellar were seen to gaze smilingly on the poor law guardian who was the victim of the blaze. Hatred was indeed great if labourers could tell Sir John Boileau, deputy Lord Lieutenant of Norfolk, to his face that 'They'd rather toss the farmers into the flames than put out a burning stack.'[24] Arson thus provided the opportunity for massive displays of collective strength and solidarity about which the authorities could do nothing.

The question as to why the fires were kindled can be a difficult one to answer, partly because so few were convicted and because no single definitive explanation is possible. The commercially-minded insurance companies made it their business to discover motives and perpetrators, the Norwich Union believing low wages and callous, unpopular farmers to be significant. The former partly explains the regional and temporal variations in incendiary activity. Fires in East Anglia peaked in November and April, the two points in the calendar when farmers decided winter and summertime wage rates. Rumours of reductions frequently brought a response in the form of a threatening letter or a warning – a box of matches lying in a bed of straw. Thus arson was an intimidatory weapon of wage bargaining when the over-supply of labour made strikes virtually impossible. Likewise, in the 1840s the behaviour of individual farmers, who had a reputation for 'grinding the poor' seems to have invited revenge. King Viall of Middleton, Suffolk, beat one of his farm boys to death, and although exonerated at the inquest he was paid a visit by an incendiary. In another case at St Nicholas Conib, Devon, a farmer caught a young girl stealing a turnip and threatened her with prosecution. The girl's mother retaliated by firing a hay stack.[25] Gleaning disputes, which were becoming frequent by the 1840s, led not only to severe injuries to gleaners but to arson as well. Other lost 'rights' produced extreme reactions. At

Milton in Cambridgeshire, single men lost their coals charity, resulting in a number of threatening letters. One warned: 'You may prepare you selfs for a fire old David yard shall be on fire nex Mondy . . . for taken me Coles.'[26] Enclosure, rare at this time, was thought to have sparked off four fires at Isleham, Cambridgeshire, in 1849.

Unemployment, together with the related issues of threshing machines and the poor law, explain much of the incendiarism. Threatening letters bear testimony to this: 'Loock at the peopel standing daley around your market place loocking you full in the face as much as to say we want worck we are starving,' ran one. 'Mr. Goose', another began, 'if you will imploy that out town man I will warm you for I think theer are single men enow in the town.' The farmers of Bluntisham, Huntingdonshire, were warned: 'We are determined to set fire to the whole of this place if you don't set us to work . . . What do you think the young men are to do if you don't set them to work . . . We must commit robbery and everything that is contrary to your wish.'[27] Employers of Irish harvesters in the east Midlands were similarly singled out for threats and fires. Threshing machines, which had been temporarily abandoned in 1830, had by the 1840s made an unpopular return to much of eastern England. The *Morning Chronicle* reported in 1844 that twenty out of thirty labourers interviewed complained bitterly of them. Nor was their antipathy necessarily limited to threshers, for farmers employing scythes and horse-drawn rakes were also fired. Unemployment forced labourers into contact with the poor law, which by the mid 1840s had been tightened up, thereby generating even greater hostility from labouring communities. It would be hard, however, to isolate the poor law as a specific cause from the wider context of rural exploitation and oppression in the manner of Foster, who reported that thirty fires had taken place on the property of poor law guardians. Many farmers fulfilled the dual role of employer and guardian, which makes the identification of the incendiary's primary grievance rather difficult.

Only a minority of the arsonists were caught and convicted, generally about one for every ten fires before 1850, though this ratio increased to one in four thereafter.[28] However, the trials of arsonists do highlight the nature and character of the crime, regarded as 'second only to murder'. The overwhelming majority of the accused, 92 per cent, were male, and of the women, domestic servants figure as the largest occupational group. In the latter cases extreme home-sickness among newly-appointed youngsters appears to have been the primary motive. These girls were taking significantly greater risks than the men, since after 1837 setting fire to an inhabited dwelling remained a capital offence when other forms of arson were not.[29] After this date, however, transportation for between ten years and life was the usual sentence, for both sexes; according to Rudé between 1840 and 1853 over 200 a year were sent to the Antipodes.[30] The average

age of the convicted was considerably younger than that of the convicted machine breakers of 1830, two-thirds being under 25 years old, and the majority described as farm labourers.[31] The study of incendiarism highlights, if nothing else, the acute social and economic plight of the young unmarrieds, especially those in their late teens who, when in work, could expect to earn only half the wage of a married man.

Arson, historians frequently caution, was not necessarily an act of protest. Between a third and a half of the East Anglian cases, Peacock asserted, were explained by 'personal Pique'; nor should pyromaniacs and insurance defrauders be ignored. [32] In eighteenth-century France 13 per cent of arsonists were given a sanity hearing, but in England one is struck by the relative absence of the insane.[33] Defrauders are undoubtedly under-represented in the criminal records, and farmers tried for the offence were invariably given the benefit of the doubt by sympathetic juries. Far more vulnerable to conviction were young children, who, being easily intimi-dated whether guilty or not, readily confessed. The spirit of imitation was motive enough for some of these young arsonists: David Jackson confessed 'he had never seen a large fire, and thought he would like to see one'. Another, a 13-year-old, had read of the Fenian outrages and thought 'he would like to be a Fenian'.[34] However, we should not overlook the fact that children from the age of 9 had work-related grievances which occasionally escalated into arson.

For tramps and vagrants the crime represented an escape from extreme hardship; indeed, many were found standing by burning stacks waiting for the police's arrival. Without food, work, or money, transportation held no fears; in fact it was seen as a merciful release.[35] The entire gamut of rural occupations had incendiaries within their ranks: policemen, postmen, weavers, blacksmiths, shoemakers, even a Sunday school teacher – nor should we overlook the possibility of political radicals, who were often the prime suspects of the reactionary gentry. One Chartist was transported for life in 1844, and the fires in the countryside around Sheffield suggest the work of trade unionists involved in industrial disputes.[36] The majority, though, were farm labourers, especially unskilled casual day workers, many of whom had worked or were still working for their victims. Men working with stock usually made their protest through maiming or sheep stealing. Incendiarism was primarily the outcome of a complete breakdown of working relations between employers and labourers over the issues of low wages and unemployment. Even where the convicted were in work, as in the case of night-watchman John Double, arson might be regarded as a means of job creation. In contrast to the Swing rioters, few of the convicted received good character references at their trials.[37] Some in East Anglia mixed their fire-raising with other criminal occupations as thieves, barn robbers, or poachers, and they would resort to the weapon of fire either to silence possible prosecutors or to wreak revenge on witnesses from earlier trials. After 1851 significant changes among the convicted occurred. Evidence from Wales and East Anglia indicates that children and tramps were prosecuted in greater numbers, which suggests that arson had become a less accurate barometer of social tensions between labourers and farmers.[38] Likewise, the evident disinclination to extinguish the fires, so prominent in the 1840s, was rarely seen in the 1850s and 1860s. By this time the young, the rural rebels, were leaving the land in greater numbers ensuring more employment for those who remained. The advent of 'high farming', together with more effective policing, led to a diminution but by no means extinction of the crime.

It is difficult to convey the fear and powerlessness experienced by the landed in the face of these nightly attacks. 'The farmers are paralysed', wrote Foster, 'they appeal to the magistrates for protection but the magistrates have no power to assist them.'[39] Unlike earlier rural disturbances no amount of yeomanry, special constables, or soldiers could halt the wave of guerilla attacks. Perpetrators could and did act with impunity, unless foolish enough to visit a stackyard when snow lay on the ground. Police, where they existed, had very little to go on; village gossip and footprints were generally the only two pieces of circumstantial evidence upon which they could act. The response from farmers and magistrates was wholly predictable. Petitions for the reintroduction of the death penalty and requests for the offer of rewards poured in to the Home Secretary. Virtually every fire in 1844 produced an offer of a reward for evidence, usually £50–100, but occasionally as much as £500. In all but three or four cases rewards went unclaimed, despite the incendiaries' indentities being well known to labouring communities. 'They were screened by the multitude', one labourer recalled; and 'they appear to be in many instances bound in a bond of secrecy', a helpless land agent complained to his employer when confronted by workmen struck suddenly with blindness, dumbness, and amnesia.[40] In one rare case where the reward was collected the couple involved were forced to flee their Suffolk village to Canada.

The newly-established rural constabularies in Bedfordshire and Norfolk proved totally inadequate, for as one Member of Parliament observed, prevention required a policeman to stand 'sentry in every homestead all night'. Occasionally metropolitan policemen sent up to the counties recorded spectacular successes, as in the case of Supt. English, who after three months dressed and working as a labourer in Suffolk, brought five arsonists to trial. Other constables, as yet uncertain of proper procedures, planted informers in cells with suspects or even hid under the table whilst the accused were interviewed by solicitors.[41] Generally speaking, the police were unsuccessful, but the wave of arson in 1844 and 1849–50 hastened the formation of police forces in West Suffolk and Cambridgeshire. Some imaginative proposals, too, were put forward: a popular one was the purchase of bloodhounds to track incendiaries. This method had been employed successfully by the Duke of Marlborough at Woodstock in Oxfordshire in 1834. One of the best, though universally ridiculed, proposals was Professor Henslow's psychological solution – firework displays. He recognized the excitement and spectacle of burning stacks and argued that if the people wanted fires, then fires they should have. Arson, once so prominent in his village of Hitcham, ceased after pyrotechnic displays on the rectory lawn.

The question remains, did arson achieve anything apart from the obvious satisfaction of causing calamity? Most farmers, after all, were insured by the mid-1830s, though landlords were slower in protecting their property. Arson was frequently self-defeating in so far as labourers lost winter work. At Stisted in Essex, fourteen men laid off as a result of fire caused 'a considerable sensation' when they marched in procession with their wives and children to the workhouse.[42] Incendiarism, however, was a double-edged weapon and the general feeling that 'fires did poor men good' was to some extent correct. Wage reductions were halted, and in 1845 came reports of farmers employing more men than were actually required. The most lasting improvement, but by no means universally applied, was the growth and spread of garden allotments. They were limited to the 'morally deserving', family men and widows while young single men received nothing.

The relationship between arson and animal maiming is an uncertain and complex one, though considerable evidence exists which suggests that arsonists displayed little concern for animal life. At one stable fire at Stonham in Suffolk the incendiary locked in six carthorses, and at another 120 sheep were burnt alive.[43] Anonymous letters refer to both arson and maiming as possible threats: 'you are trettened to be burned,' a Norfolk farmer was warned, 'and as shure as it is spoke it will be done and very soon. By your corn or Cattle and there is a fresh plan to destroye your sheep.' In another case a labourer named Wright weighed the alternatives of firing a stack or 'sticking' a sheep. He chose the former.[44] Moreover, some farmers fell victim to a tripartite crescendo of property attacks. Asplen, a farmer of Bluntisham in Huntingdonshire, had all his gates damaged and his horses' manes and tails cut off before losing a barn and stackyard through fire. More extreme was the case of a Northamptonshire squire who found first his pheasants dead, then his dogs poisoned, and finally his manor house razed to the ground.[45]

As a crime of protest, animal maiming was of a different order to that of incendiarism in terms of scale, frequency, and motive. Historians have all too frequently assumed it to epitomize rural protest, but recent research indicates that care needs to be taken in both identifying the type of animal maimed and the method employed before drawing conclusions.[46] But whatever the motive, maimers exercised a powerful psychological terror over farmers who did not always care to advertise themselves as victims of these 'fiendish outrages'. As with arson, maiming became more common after the defeat of Swing, again indicating the new bitterness in social relations. It carried on rising through the 1830s, peaking in 1837 and again in the incendiary year of 1844, the worst year on record, when forty-three stood trial in England and Wales.[47] Geographically it was widespread, with the counties of Devon, Somerset, Staffordshire, and Yorkshire experiencing high levels; but as in most things criminal it was an East Anglian speciality. What makes maiming so difficult to understand, contemporary reticence apart, is that so few were convicted. It was the dark crime of the countryside.

Legally, maiming was not primarily a matter of cruelty to animals, an offence that came to be covered by the far less severe Cruelty to Animals Act of 1822, but with malicious damage to property. A man called Pearce was saved from the gallows in 1789 when he was tried for thrusting a stick through a cow, it transpiring that he had become angry with the animal when it had resisted his amorous advances. Pearce received a lesser sentence for attempting bestiality.[48] Such an incident was clearly devoid of class hatred, a point which has to be borne in mind when surveying other cases. Gangs killed horses with a view to buying carcasses for dog meat, and 'wanton levity' was a good enough defence to acquit murderous horsemen. Donkey killing invariably resulted from feuds between labouring men. More incomprehensible are the large numbers of horses which met death through poisoning in the arable regions of the country. George Ewart Evans's oral histories of the horsemen's pride and dedication for their charges make this a paradoxical puzzle.[49] The answer to this, however, lies in grooming, particularly the horsemen's desire to achieve a 'bloom' or shine on the horse's coat. In East Anglia this was done using secret recipes, handed down from one generation of horsekeepers to the next, recipes which contained poisonous, though not necessarily fatal, ingredients, notably arsenic and brake root. This would explain the sudden disappearance of inexperienced young horsemen after their teams had died under mysterious circumstances. Variations of the practice can be found outside East Anglia; for example, in Godalming, Surrey, where a horse died of suffocation because an egg had lodged in its throat. The paper reported: 'It is too well known that the country fellows . . . have ever been addicted to give their horses eggs . . . with the silly view of making their coats finer than can be obtained from good corn or good rubbing.'[50]

Misplaced care and affection, however, explains only a minority of animal killings. Discovering the motives behind the remaining majority is an impossible task – only thirty-one convicted maimers were transported to the Antipodes. Occasionally, however, the maimer left behind a threatening letter or made a defiant speech from the dock which allows us an insight. William Watts is a case in point. In bitter speech at his trial for shooting six horses and cattle at Buxton, Norfolk, he complained

> to such a state had they brought the poor of this country by oppressing them with taxes, poor rates . . . it was impossible for a poor man to live by honest means, and all this was to support big-gutted relieving officers, and other folks connected with them and the unions.[51]

In another case, Edmund Botwright, a member of a notorious gang who were responsible for the first murder of a Suffolk policeman, left a threatening letter to his employer after he had hanged two bullocks. In it he complained of the use of machinery, and he ended by warning:

> You bloody farmer could not live it was not for the poore,
> tis them that kepe you bluddy raskells alive, but their
> will be a slauter made amongst you verry soone. I shood
> verry well like to hang you the same as I hanged your
> beastes You bluddy rogue I will lite up a little fire for
> you this first opertunity that I can make.[52]

The element of social protest can only be guessed at in most cases where animals were subjected to a range of tortures and lingering deaths. As a general rule the smaller the animal the easier it was to maim in large quantities at a single stroke. Sheep were particularly vulnerable to mass slaughter. At Manea, Cambridgeshire, fifty-one sheep were driven into a ditch and drowned, a method much favoured in the Fens. Later, with the advent of the railways, 107 sheep were penned in on the track in an incident at Downham. Where the maimer's attention was focused on only a few animals the slaughter took on a bloody, brutal, and noisy character. Cattle and horses were run through with pitchforks, their genitalia cut or torn in shreds, eyes gouged out, or their legs hamstrung.[53] Such incidents suggest that the nadir of social relations between employers and labourers had been reached.

Economically powerless, and in the words of one farmer, 'oppressed wonderfully', the farm labourers of much of southern and eastern England were not without the means of redress. The defeat of the 'Last Labourers' Revolt' of 1830, rather then marking the end of the rural war set off a new, more vicious, covert, and sustained struggle by labourers. The weapons, too, were more varied, although arson, maiming, and threatening letters proved the most effective in their arsenal. The silence of deferential, forelocking Hodge was broken only by the crackle of burning timber and straw and the death cries of mutilated animals.

Notes

1 Heath, 1978, 44.
2 Wells, 1979, 115–39: Wells 1981, 514–30: Charlesworth, 1980, 101–11; Archer, 1982a, 277–84; Rule, 1986, 354–6.
3 de Montmorency, 1902, 33.
4 Hobsbawm and Rudé, 1973, 56.
5 ibid., 32; Lowerson, 1982, 55–82; Wells, 1985, 143–4.
6 Jones, 1976a, 6–7.
7 *Journal of the Statistical Society of London*, 1845, 353; Glyde, 1856b, 234.
8 Coleman, 1844, 63; *Fraser's Magazine*, 1844, 245.
9 Thompson, 1968, 233–5.
10 Bowley, 1898, 702–22.
11 Peacock, 1974, 32.
12 *The Times*, 16 July 1844.
13 ibid., 4 July 1844; Digby, 1978, 115–18.
14 *The Times*, 21 June 1844, 26 January 1844.
15 Rudé, 1978, 16; Jones, 1981, 572.
16 Caird, 1968, 467–8.
17 *The Times*, 8 May 1844, 21 June 1844, 28 August 1844, 7 September 1844.
18 Norwich Union Fire Office Minutes, 18 September 1850.
19 Archer, 1982b, 183–4.
20 *The Times*, 25 May 1844.
21 *Morning Chronicle*, 30 July 1844.
22 *Hansard*, 12 June 1844.
23 Jones, 1976a, 19; *The Times*, 8 April 1844.
24 ibid., 25 July 1844; Norfolk RO 69 117x6, 16 December 1851.
25 Jones, 1976a, 11; *The Times*, 10 September 1844.
26 Peacock, 1974, 58; Harber, 1975, 39.
27 Jones, 1976a, 30; *Norfolk Chronicle*, 29 November 1845; *The Times*, 22 March 1844.
28 Archer, 1982c, 89.
29 Archer, 1982b, 281–2.
30 Rudé, 1978, 252.
31 Hobsbawm and Rudé, 1973, 209; Jones, 1976a, 20.
32 Peacock, 1974, 30–3.
33 Abbiateci, 1978, 160.
34 Archer, 1982b, 276–80.
35 Archer, 1982c, 90.
36 Rudé, 1978, 149; *The Times*, 8 July 1844.
37 Jones, 1976a, 19–20.
38 Archer, 1982b, 285–6; Jones, 1977, *passim*.
39 *The Times*, 20 May 1844.
40 Glyde, 1894, 46; East Sussex RO, Ashburnham Papers, HA1/HB6/1b/62, 2 July 1844.
41 *Hansard*, 22 March 1844; Jones, 1976a, 18; *Bury and Norwich Post*, 25 June 1845.
42 *The Times*, 27 June 1844.
43 Archer, 1985, 155.
44 PRO HO 40/29(2), 1831; Archer, 1985, 156.
45 *The Times*, 10 January 1844; Hobsbawm and Rudé, 1973, 247.
46 Archer, 1985, 147–57.
47 Rudé, 1978, 17.

48 Radzinowicz, 1948, 67.
49 Evans, 1960, *passim*.
50 Archer, 1985, 153; *Bury and Norwich Post*, 18 June 1823.
51 Peacock, 1974, 59.
52 Archer, 1985, 155.
53 ibid., 150–2.

6

Landowners and the rural community

F. M. L. Thompson

As the twentieth century knows very well, it is not too difficult for any tolerably well-organized and disciplined group in authority, adequately furnished with jackboots, machine guns, and bully boys, to hold the populace in thrall, extracting an outward show of respect and obedience from the inward experience of fear. One strand in the rural literature of the nineteenth century asserts, or implies, that rural communities were held in thrall to the superior and possessing classes through the exercise of analogous coercive power and the fear of the consequences of disobedience, even though these might be exercised in a more decentralized, more 'civilized', and less obtrusive fashion. It is a view which sees agricultural labourers and village folk harbouring a sullen resentment, dislike, and hatred of farmers, parsons, and squires, nurtured on poverty, oppression, and regimentation, which for most of the time slumbered and grumbled under the surface, and occasionally flashed out in explosions of violent words or deeds at moments of acute crisis.[1] The idea of the undeclared war of the countryside with scarcely veiled jackboot social relationships is vividly expressed in a well-known passage by Joseph Arch:

> We labourers had no lack of lords and masters. There were the parson and his wife at the rectory. There was the squire, with his hand of iron overshadowing us all. There was no velvet glove on that hard hand, as many a poor man found to his hurt . . . At the sight of the squire the people trembled. He lorded it right feudally over his tenants, the farmers; the farmers in their turn tyrannised over the labourers; the labourers were no better than toads under a harrow. Most of the farmers were oppressors of the poor; they put on the iron wage-screw, and screwed the labourers' wages down, down below the living point; they stretched him on the rack of life-long abject poverty.[2]

A second view portrays the rural relationship not so much as one of conflict contained by coercion, as of potential disaffection or awkward independence massaged away by social leadership, social conditioning, and paternalism. In this version the underlying relationship is also one of conflict, but vigilance and calculated manipulation on the part of the gentry normally succeeded in mediating it into an outward social harmony resting on deference and obedience, although periodically the conflict broke surface in protests, riots, or strikes.[3] A third view, singing the praises of the happy harmony of village life, of simple thatched-cottage contentment nourished by landlord kindliness, is barely credible in the light of today's conviction that all societies function with tensions and frictions, but was nevertheless widely held by contemporary apologists for the existing social order.[4]

The attraction of all these views is that, in their different ways, they present the relationship between landowners and the rural community in a satisfactorily positive way, involve the attribution of clear-cut, strongly motivated, and purposive actions to the landowners and equally clear-cut and intelligible responses from the villagers, and lead on into making abstractions about social control or class collaboration. The difficulty with them is that they rest on assumptions about landowners' behaviour and attitudes, and precisely about the extent to which the effects of their actions were calculated and intended, and about the degree to which they felt any commitment or involvement – whether defensive or benevolent – with the rural community at large, that make the theories conveniently self-validating. There were certainly many individual landowners whose sense of the duties and responsibilities of their station led them to minister to the moral and material welfare of what they thought of as their people, in ways which they decided were most suitable and proper, discharging what was felt to be the pastoral care of their flock so as to condition, discipline, perhaps control, the recipients of attention and mould them into dutiful, God-fearing, obedient, industrious, useful, law-abiding, and quiescent people who knew their place, kept it, and did not question the social order which made it a humble one. There were also, no doubt, a few who did similar things more explicitly out of fear of social disorder and rural unrest, conceiving the effects of their actions on the minds and lives of the community as measures or moral police in support of formal civil authority. But many more, the silent majority as it were, were not sufficiently active, imaginative, responsible or assertive to try to use their power and position to influence the rural community in any systematic way. They were narrowly self-centred in their interpretation of what was required to protect their interests, they were concerned to look after their own ease and comfort, to keep up appearances, and to look after their immediate dependants; beyond the park walls, figuratively, if not indifferent to wider issues of the social order in the countryside and how best to preserve it, they did not regard it as their business to make any special contribution. Those who could not be bothered much with the schools, churches, reading rooms, sick clubs, soup kitchens, drinking places, or recreations of the lower orders were the saving grace of the rural community. It was their indifference, quite as much as the inability of the methods of social control, if there was indeed such a deliberate effort at social management, to achieve their proposed ends, which preserved the capacity of the rural population for independent development. Liberty, after all, depends not only on eternal vigilance, but also on eternal sloth and inefficiency in the part of those with power and privilege.

Sloth, however, was not exactly what farmers and labourers felt to be the hallmark of the preservation of game, which was the most widespread and most rapidly growing country pursuit of the greatest number of landowners, the activity which more than any other made country life and the ownership of country estates gratifying, and the point at which landowners mobilized their maximum amount of directly coercive power and displayed most nakedly the legal and physical force which maintained the rights of the propertied over the propertyless in the countryside. A Scottish tenant farmer might 'call a gamekeeper's work doing nothing; the principal part of his business is tormenting the tenants . . . I say that gamekeeping is an idle trade and an idle class of men go into it,' but he meant not that gamekeepers were indolent but that they were interfering busybodies engaged in an unjustifiable, unproductive, and vexatious activity.[5] The systematic preservation of game, the employment of armies of keepers, the formation of special game departments in the managerial structure of large estates, the controlled and costly rearing of birds and the provision of special coverts for them to inhabit, the organization of large shooting parties, and the culminating attainment of grand *battues* where the hundreds or thousands of brace were carefully noted in the game record books, were essentially Victorian developments. As the earlier, more informal and less effective shooting of game that was wild-bred and not too thick on the ground developed into the formal Victorian shoot, with its improved shotguns, regular shooting attire, and increased numbers, landowners took increasing trouble to protect their stake in cash and in pleasure. The custodians of these investments multiplied, from about 8,000 at the beginning of Victoria's reign to over 17,000 at its end. In the rural districts there were, by 1911, more than twice as many gamekeepers as country policemen;[6] the popular impression, in any case, was that the rural police helped at public expense in the struggle to keep poachers away from private preserves, an impression which the 1862 Night Poaching Act did nothing to allay. It may well be that this Act, which gave the police powers to search on suspicion of poaching, was passed at the request of the chief constables who were alarmed at the growing number of bloody affrays between poachers and keepers, and wanted firmer legal grounds on which the police could intervene to keep the peace by anticipating such conflicts;[7] that did not alter the fact that the police appeared to be assisting the keepers in putting down poaching, rather than engaging in the neutral task of preventing bloodshed and murder.

The ordinary countrymen's view was that of Joseph Arch: 'They object very much to being subjected at any time to be assailed by a police officer and searched; they do not like that idea of the law.'[8] The Act was looked on as blatantly discriminatory class legislation, since it was only the poor man on foot with bulging pockets who was liable to be searched, not the gentleman in his carriage; and it, and the whole parcel of game laws to which it was but a refinement, were regarded as draconian and unjust since wild animals ought not to be, and could not become, private property. Arch again expressed the general view: 'We labourers do not believe hares and rabbits belong to any individual, not any more than thrushes and blackbirds do.'[9] He was quite right in law: the offence in poaching was in trespassing on private land in pursuit of game, not in the mere taking of a wild animal that could not have a legal owner. Such niceties did not make the game laws any more acceptable. They were generally held in contempt by countrymen, who failed to see anything morally reprehensible about poaching, and who regarded poachers as heroes or resourceful and daring hunters who brought valuable and tasty food to meagre larders, not as villains, criminals, or sinners. Poachers themselves, apart from the professional gangs who lived by supplying the urban markets with illicit game, and which were thought to be particularly active and well-organized in the 1820s and 1860s, were the braver and more independent village men, who regarded themselves at one level as engaging in a battle of wits with the keepers, at another level as fighting a secret, just war against the tyrannical selfishness of the wealthy.[10] For once the radical politicians who denounced the game laws, from John Bright in 1845 to Joseph Chamberlain in 1885, were voicing a deeply felt grievance of genuine countrymen rather than expressing an urban radical's notion of what countrymen ought to be feeling.

There was no respect for the game laws, and gamekeepers were disliked and detested by farmers and labourers alike. Here was one way in which the landowners were doing what they could to unite the rest of the rural community against them. 'Gamekeepers are generally troublesome to farmers,' said a Norfolk farmer from one of the most highly preserved and most favoured sporting regions in the country, 'breaking down fences, leaving gates open, prowling about. They are generally men of bad character.' Clare Sewell Read, a Norfolk MP, confirmed that 'gamekeepers are generally very much disliked by farmers'.[11] The interference by the keepers was one irritant; the interference by the hares, rabbits, and gamebirds themselves was another, breeding a long story of protests against crop damage and loss, which were reduced but not stilled by the Gladstonian 1880 Ground Game Act that gave tenant farmers the right to take hares and rabbits on their own holdings. If the evil repute and bad blood caused by game laws and gamekeepers are not to be doubted, however, the extent to which these infected the countryside is still worth examining. All regions, all climates, and all types of farmland and woodland were not equally suited to game or equally favoured by sportsmen. Grouse were partial only to the bare, uncultivated moors and fells of the northern uplands and the highland zones; they shared some of the bleaker and more remote parts of the kingdom with deer, for whose stalking men were already prepared to pay as much as £2,000 a week by the 1870s.[12] In these thinly populated and infertile parts there was little competition with agriculture and little contact with communities except for those who lived by gillying; there were vivid folk-tales of brutal clearances of poor crofting families to make way for the deer, but the actual culprits were more often sheep. It was in the lowland areas that game and people came together, and here the partridge and pheasant needed ploughland and grain crops while hares and rabbits, though ubiquitous, thrived best on light and well-drained soils. The sporting map followed landowners' tastes as well as natural habitats, and hence the distribution of game preservation observed man-made as well as natural contours. It shows that preservation, and therefore the community's experience of game laws and keepers, varied widely from one part of the country to another.

The gamekeeping force, and hence presumably game preservation, reached its peak in the early 1900s, a fitting reflection of the opulent pursuit of amusement in the Edwardian countryside. The 60 per cent growth in the number of keepers since the 1860s is perhaps surprising, across the years of depression; but it suggests the switch from basic agricultural production towards the provision of leisure activities as the role of the land, and emphasizes the degree to which shooting rents supplemented or surpassed farm rents as sources of income from land in some areas. It is no surprise that, in 1911, predominantly rural and agricultural counties such as Hereford, Norfolk, Suffolk, Dorset, Shropshire, and Westmorland had twenty to thirty gamekeepers to every 10,000 inhabitants, while highly urbanized and industrialized counties like Middlesex, Lancashire, Durham, or the West Riding had only one or two keepers per 10,000 population, since this is simply a slightly eccentric way of measuring the difference between rural and urban communities.[13] It is of more significance that the heavily keepered counties also had six or seven times as many keepers per head of total population as did other almost equally agricultural counties such as Leicester, Cheshire, Essex, or the East Riding, and over three times as many as deeply rural Cornwall, Devon, Lincoln, and Bedford. Keepers, however, in so far as they were not merely private policemen, were more concerned with the population of game animals in their charge than with the size of the local human population, and a more functional measure of their presence is their relation to land areas as the basic determinant of game population. On this scale Suffolk, at the top, with ten keepers per 10,000 acres of land in the county, had over five times the keeper density of Cornwall, at the bottom. The densely keepered areas, on this reckoning, were Norfolk, Suffolk, Hampshire, Hertford, Surrey, Sussex, Berkshire, Dorset, Kent, and Shropshire; the agricultural counties where keepers were comparatively sparse, less than half as common as in the strongly guarded counties, were Northampton, Huntingdon, the East Riding, Devon, Leicester, Cumberland, Cambridge, Westmorland, Lincoln, and Cornwall. A similar analysis can be made for the Welsh counties, where only Flint, Anglesey, and Denbigh had high scores on the Suffolk or Hereford level, and all the other counties, most noticeably Brecon, Merioneth, Carmarthen, and Cardigan, were thinly keepered on the Cornish model.

Both measures confirm the supremacy of Norfolk and Suffolk as shooting counties where there were three or four gamekeepers in every village, and they outnumbered the police by two or three to one; here the iron of the game laws and the bitterness of the keepers' war was likely to have entered most deeply into village life. The home counties, perhaps, required particularly strong protection to ward off marauding Londoners, and if they are set aside in a special category the other most popular preserving areas with high rates of contact with keepers were Hampshire, Hereford, Dorset, and Shropshire, closely followed by Sussex, and with a large group of middling counties headed by Buckingham and Oxford. Much of the best hunting country of the midland shires – Northampton, Leicester, Nottingham – had low keepering ratios, because foxes and pheasants were not compatible, and enthusiasm for the one tended to exclude the other.[14] Otherwise there was no special logic about the distribution of the under-keepered areas: there were some in the south-west, in the east, in the west Midlands, the east Midlands, the north-west, and the north-east, in most cases rubbing shoulders with highly preserved counties; there was no particular correlation with the presence or absence or aristocratic or gentry estates. If, however, it is assumed that one gamekeeper could manage about 1,000 acres with efficient care and protection of game, and perhaps twice that area with something short of perfection, then the figures mean that in more than half the counties of England and Wales, comprising nearly two-thirds of the countryside, at least half the fields and woods never knew the attentions of gamekeepers. It is a fair guess that some very large proportion, approaching half, of the rural population also never encountered gamekeepers or needed to take careful steps to avoid them.

There is some evidence that the regional contrasts, already apparent in the mid-Victorian years, became more marked in the later nineteenth century; in 1861 individual counties ranged 50 per cent above and below the national mean of keepers per 10,000 acres, while by 1911 the variance had grown to over 100 per cent. The widening differences were perhaps due to improved upper-class railway mobility that encouraged specialization on the best endowed and most favoured areas, perhaps to expansion of shooting in the counties most affected by falling grain prices, perhaps simply to the quirks of individual tastes. As a straw in the wind, Cheshire, a dairying county which maintained its agricultural prosperity, marked time in its appointment of keepers and dropped from the premier position in 1861, more closely watched even than Norfolk, to a middling position in 1911. It is likely, therefore, that what had been a general if somewhat thinly spread experience in the mid-Victorian years, became a much more localized and concentrated confrontation in the later nineteenth century. Perceptions of the inequity of the game laws became more vivid just at the time that practical encounters with their enforcement were becoming less typical.

The shooting gentry pursued the protection of their pleasures with no less zest than they devoted to the shooting itself, heedless of the social cost. That cost included the spread of animosity, encouragement of contempt for the law, and threats to public order; it also included the fostering of a popular poaching culture which lived on pub stories of daring feats, narrow escapes, and cunning ruses which outwitted gamekeepers, which embodied the local lore of the virtues of living independently and defying authority, and whose standards were those of the superiority of the rights of free men to take free, natural goods over the rights of private property.[15] The keenest shots, game preservers, and employers of keepers would have argued, no doubt, that their sport was such an integral part of landowning, and indeed constituted the chief benefit and reward from the possession of landed estates, that any hostility and alienation engendered by its full and proper enjoyment, although naturally misguided and regrettable, had to be accepted and countered just as any other anti-landlord tendencies were to be countered – by leadership, example, education, and Christian morality.

It is nevertheless one of the ironies of the countryside that the ardent game preservers, who had strong motives for residence on their estates and intimate knowledge of their locality which should have nourished close ties with the local community, in fact made a major contribution to creating friction and inflaming passions. Hunting, that other sporting interest which brought landowners into the country, was generally held not to produce similar socially divisive effects, except among the ranks of the upper class themselves where foxhunter and game preserver were not infrequently at loggerheads. Great trouble and offence could be caused when either fox or pheasant was killed outside the ordained course of pleasurable pursuit, and preserving landlords who took stern measures to exclude the hunt from their properties and to destroy the foxes were likely to attract pungently expressed local disfavour. This conflict was never general, partly because there was to some extent a separation of hunting and shooting areas, and mainly because many sporting landowners both hunted and shot, either in succession on different days in the week or in succession in different stages in life, taking to shooting as they became too old and portly to continue riding to hounds. Where it did break out, however, the conflict could be decidedly sharp, rising to its peak in the early 1900s as the enormous Edwardian shooting parties mounted to a crescendo of slaughter and were bitterly blamed for a growing scarcity of foxes. The hunting community, with its effortless assumption of prior and superior rights, denied responsibility for causing these frictions which disrupted the solidarity of the landed classes and complicated, if they did not frustrate, the task of keeping rural society in order. Hunting literature, indeed, especially hunting fiction, gave a strong impression that there was a real hunting community, cutting across class lines, bringing together the rural classes, and acting as an important agent of social harmony. There is abundant evidence that many farmers regularly rode to hounds, from the wealthy Yarborough estate tenants who hunted with the Brocklesby in the late nineteenth century to the hundreds of Leicestershire farmers with the Quorn, and the Gloucestershire farmers who virtually controlled the running of the Vale of White Horse.[16] It was certainly not a gentry preserve or a male preserve – unlike shooting – but apart from local farmers and large numbers of outsiders who flocked to the fashionable hunts, it is not clear that other social groups were much represented; country doctors and parsons maybe, but the hunting village blacksmith or carrier must have been a rarity, and other village workers, let alone farm labourers, were hardly in the hunt. If it is more than doubtful whether hunting was an all-class affair for rural society, its close dependence on a landlord–farmer axis was of considerable importance in bringing together those two groups which otherwise were socially distanced and liable to have some conflicting economic interests. Certainly some farmers were obliged by the terms of their tenancies to support the local hunt, by walking hound puppies and by allowing the hunt over their fields; and others showed their discontent at the considerable damage to fences and growing crops that a field of hundreds of horses could easily cause, by exercising their right to warn the hunt off their farms. These, however, were a minority; eased by the diplomacy and cash of hunt committees, and by masters of foxhounds who gave annual dinners to the farmers, paid some compensation for damages, and took trouble to cultivate friendly relations, hunting enjoyed the goodwill and support of the majority of farmers, without which it could not have existed. As for the majority of the local community, labourers may have derived some pleasure from the colourful spectacle of the meet, or a glimpse of a large field at full stretch, and relished the chance that persons of high degree might be levelled by falling into ditches, but at best they were bystanders with no place in the hunting network, and the goings on of the hunting folk did not affect them one way or the other.

In the eyes of the generality of landowners the function of their estates was to provide the income to support their lifestyle; the function of the countryside was to provide good sport. If the sport was hunting, it did something to unite the upper reaches of rural society, bringing together landlords and tenants, and at least did nothing to antagonize the labourers. If it was shooting, on the other hand, it emphasized and exacerbated social divisions, irritating the tenant-farmers and imbuing the labourers, who felt the direct consequences of game preservation and game laws, with a sense of social injustice and a contempt for the law which the wealthy used to oppress the poor. In such a situation the rational and efficient behaviour for the landowners as a class would have been to make sure that in those regions where their own actions tended most to undermine social order and their own authority, counter-measures designed to neutralize such influences were most actively promoted. Direct strengthening of the power of the law by maintaining more rural police in the disturbed than in the quiet areas was one possibility. Such a course was indeed implicit in the advice of the chief constables of rural counties in 1859, whose figures of savage attacks on gamekeepers not surprisingly showed a clear correlation with the main game preserving counties.[17] It was not, however, followed in practice. It was true that in 1861, when county police forces had not been long established and many were still in their first few years of feeling their way towards a desired size, the leading game and poaching county, Norfolk, had marginally more policemen per head of population than a hunting county like Leicestershire; but it was scarcely a significant difference that could suggest any deliberate reinforcement of coercive power.[18] In the next fifty years, as game preservation intensified and became more elaborate, the numbers of rural police were everywhere increased; but they did not increase as fast as total population, and in the great shooting counties police forces expanded markedly less than elsewhere. The result was that by 1911 policing ratios were practically identical in all the more agricultural counties, with only Cornwall, Rutland, and Shropshire apparently more law-abiding than the rest in so far as they had one third fewer policemen in relation to the population than the others. East Anglia functioned with exactly the same policing ratio as the great hunting shires, and indeed of the ten counties where gamekeepers were thickest on the ground only three – Hertfordshire, Kent, and Surrey – had a high police presence, twice that of the other seven, and that was accounted for by their large urban populations and proximity to London. There had clearly been no effort to match heavy concentrations of gamekeepers with heavy concentrations of police to contain the extra lawlessness engendered by strict preservation; rather, the reverse had happened, and the great shooting landowners, by multiplying the number of keepers they employed at least by two, had enabled their counties to economize on police, patrolling their covers with their own staff, perhaps consciously in order to avoid the unpopularity of being responsible for putting more policemen on the public rates.[19]

Such figures might suggest that it was no more difficult to keep order in the areas of greatest exposure to the game war than anywhere else. Conceivably contemporary opinion exaggerated the popular hostility to the game laws and sympathy with the poachers, and there was never any particular problem in maintaining authority and landowner superiority in the affected areas, but this seems unlikely in the light of the clear-cut testimony. It is possible that the resentment was indeed widespread, but remained sullen rather than overt because of other pressures which were effective without there being any need for the display of extra physical force. Among such influences education took pride of place as the panacea prescribed by Victorians in authority when they sensed any whiff of social or moral decay or collapse in the populace, and was indeed frequently regarded as a more effective and enduring instrument of social order than troops, police, or magistrates. Support of village schools was one of the most typical activities of Victorian landowners, and the visit to the school-room, more often by the lady than the master of the big house, was the most common form of contact of the possessing classes with the lower orders apart from the ranks of immediate employees and dependants, at least with the younger members of the community. Support was typical, but not universal. It is not in doubt that before 1870, when popular education depended on the voluntary schools, these were two or three times more numerous, in relation to the population of school age, in the rural and agricultural than in the urban and industrial areas; this meant that rural communities subscribed more generously than urban ones to the building of schools. Which members of rural communities subscribed is, however, in some doubt; and while there were considerable variations in school provision among the predominantly agricultural counties them-selves, it is more than doubtful whether these variations conformed to any scale of differing degrees of exposure to the risks of disaffection.

The history of education has been so preoccupied with questions of policy that the geography of schools has not been much studied. Kay-Shuttleworth's view on the extreme educational backwardness of East Anglia in the 1830s, where he found little except 'a lawless population of paupers, disbanded smugglers and poachers', may be only a small straw in the wind, since on his way to becoming the country's leading educational pundit he was biased towards noticing whatever proved the need for more schools; it does not look, however, as if the shooting squires were at this time aware of any particular call to concern themselves with educating the people.[20] A generation later the Newcastle Commission on Popular Education provided a more objective measure of the variations between counties in the support of voluntary schools, when in 1861 it published a table ranking the counties in order of the proportion of children on the books of their schools in relation to total population. This has been accepted 'as an index of the eagerness or reluctance with which local persons were prepared to subscribe to the building of the schools'.[21] After twenty-five years of considerable effort and achievement by the voluntary societies, during which the numbers and capacity of their schools had been increased four- or five-fold, this index recorded that the greatest eagerness had been shown by Wiltshire, Westmorland, Oxfordshire, and Rutland, and the most reluctance by Cornwall, Northumberland, Warwickshire, and Durham; the best performers were nearly three times more generous than the worst in finding funds for school building. The table does not distinguish between rural and urban areas, and it is arguable that the educationally neglected counties were predominantly those with large industrial and urban populations: Lancashire, Yorkshire, Nottinghamshire, and Staffordshire did not appear far from the bottom of the league. On the other hand, decidedly rural and agricultural counties might be either very keen on schools, like Wiltshire and Westmorland, or definitely unenthusiastic, like Worcestershire and Devonshire; while the indifferent to mediocre performance of Norfolk, Suffolk, Hampshire, or Sussex suggests that the strong shooting interests of those counties had still seen no need to show any special interest in rural schools. They were indeed comfortably outclassed by the great hunting shires, all of which supported more schools. Hence, if there was any connection at all between the sport-based social characteristics and needs of a district, and the level of interest in and support for schools, it seems possible that the greater friendliness, neighbourliness, and comparative absence of social friction in the hunting shires, and indeed in counties not notable for any kind of sport, disposed the propertied classes to an active interest in the educational welfare of their communities, while the frictions and disaffections of the shooting counties, far from causing the landed gentry acute anxieties about the local moral order and inducing special zeal for carefully managed schools as a corrective, served to make them tight-fisted, suspicious, uncooperative, or even hostile towards the idea of helping ungrateful and disaffected people to better themselves.

In the final phase of voluntary activity, before rate-financed schools established effective control of elementary education, it is possible that the landowners in some of the previously laggard areas were shamed or provoked into making good some of their earlier neglect and indifference. Leaving aside those cases where there was a stampede after 1870 to safeguard Anglican and paternalist interests by hastily founding new National Society schools within the few years' grace allowed by the Act, in order to ward off the threat that school boards would be set up to provide for local deficiencies of school places, there is some evidence of more sustained efforts. By the end of the 1880s the dust had more or less settled on the controversies over the establishment of school boards, and where none had been set up, either compulsorily or voluntarily, it is safe to assume that the voluntary schools were adequate in size and quality and were tolerably well supported by the communities. In 1889 school boards looked after the education of 62 per cent of the population of England, but there were extremely wide regional variations in their distribution: 95 per cent of the population of Middlesex came under school boards, and 80 per cent in Surrey and Warwickshire, but only 3 per cent in Rutland and 10 per cent in Dorset. Many of the counties which, by this standard, had the poorest record of support for voluntary schools merely confirmed the indifference that they had already demonstrated by 1861: thus Devon, Cornwall, Durham, Nottinghamshire, Yorkshire, and Staffordshire were at the bottom of the 1889 league just as they had been towards the bottom of the 1861 table. Similarly, Rutland and Dorset, Berkshire, Hertfordshire, Oxfordshire, and Wiltshire appear at the top of both tables. There were, however, some counties in which an apparently sharp change in attitude towards voluntary schools occurred between 1861 and 1889: there seems to have been a notable increase in the liberality with which schools were supported in Cheshire, Herefordshire, and Shropshire, that had transformed them from middling to poor performers in 1861 into front runners in 1889; and while Lancashire, Northumberland, and Worcestershire reached the middle of the order only in 1889, they had moved up from very lowly positions. On the other hand, support seems to have contracted severely in Gloucestershire, which dropped from ninth to thirtieth place, and to have dwindled significantly in Essex, Northamptonshire, Norfolk, and Westmorland, whose relative standings deteriorated markedly.[22]

The regional pattern of concern for education is an interesting one, not least for its failure to conform with the distribution of large or gentry estates, or with distinctions between pastoral and cereal areas, let alone with distinctions between hunting and shooting counties. Since it also shows, albeit tentatively, that it was possible both for counties which cared about schools and those which did not to manage with unusually small numbers of rural police, it suggests that education did not necessarily turn out the superior law-abiding citizenry it was intended to produce. It is, above all, an awkward pattern for any thesis which places landowner support at the centre of Anglican school expansion or regards an interest in the village school as a typical landowner activity. The implication that landowners as a group were erratic, unsystematic, and unreliable in their concern for local schools, however, accords well with the opinions of contemporary administrators, who saw the local parson as the key figure in initiating and sustaining the local school, and the local landowners as a set of potential but reluctant subscribers which the clergy had to struggle hard to mobilize. The conclusion of the assistant commissioner for the eastern counties, reporting to the Newcastle Commission on Popular Education, was that

> Farmers seldom feel any interest in the school, and seldom therefore subscribe to it. Landowners are often non-resident, and if they subscribe, do so to a very insufficient amount. Where landowners are resident and study the welfare of their tenants and labourers, they usually take an interest in the school and contribute liberally, if they do not wholly support it. But these cases are not frequent.

The assistant commissioner investigating a sample of parishes in the western agricultural counties found more than a third of the local landowners 'to whom the school in the parish from which they derive their income is a simple matter of unconcern'. The Newcastle *Report* itself summed up the situation in a passage which was sternly critical of the landowners:

> [The clergyman] is the man who most feels the mischief arising from want of education . . . He begs from the landowners; if he fails to persuade them to take their fair share of the burden, he begs from his friends, and even from strangers; and at last submits more meritoriously, and most generously, to bear not only his own proportion of the expense, but also that which ought to be borne by others. It has been repeatedly noticed by the school inspectors, and it is our duty to state that as a class the landowners, especially those who are non-resident (though there are many honourable exceptions) do not do their duty in the support of popular education, and that they allow others, who are far less able to afford it, to bear the burden of their neglect.[23]

On this view the regional and chronological variations are to be explained largely in terms of the chance distribution of zealous, conscientious, and persuasive clergymen rather than in terms of differences between landowners in their perceptions of their self-interest or their ideas of their social responsibilities. The often passive role of landowners is a warning that the frequent references in family and estate papers to annual subscriptions of a few guineas to local schools are not to be taken as evidence of active involvement, but may more likely indicate no more than a token, and often perfunctory, compliance with the importunings of the local clergymen. The school managers, and of course the parson, would be well aware of which local landowners did subscribe and which did not, and the annual subscription was no doubt a small price to pay for securing freedom from vexatious calls, and a reputation for basic attention to a social duty, and as such served to smooth relations with that level of rural society. Those at the receiving end of education, however, the schoolchildren and their parents, are most unlikely to have known who the subscribers were, so that simple subscription offered no dividends of deference or obligation to the landowner, and provided him with no paternalist satisfaction. Active involvement, of a kind likely to be noticed by the villagers and to reinforce their attachment to the local gentry, required considerably more effort: the donation of a site, financing of the school building, or support of the teacher's salary were the material contributions likely to accompany a keen and continuing interest in a school and to bring a patron into direct and impressionable contact with the children. Many landowners did indeed contribute on this scale, like Lord Shaftesbury, who within three months of inheriting the family estate in Dorset had launched three schools where before there were none, and ended by meeting the salaries of six or seven school masters and mistresses; less pious peers did no less, like the Duke of Bedford, Lord Pembroke in Wiltshire, or Lord Cholmondeley in Norfolk. The example, however, was far from widespread. A sample of seven recent volumes of the *Victoria County History* mentions 118 National Society schools; 68 of these apparently had no particular patron worthy of mention, while of those which were substantially supported by individuals only 21, or 17 per cent of the total, had patrons from the landowning classes.[24] This is probably a reasonable measure of the extent of serious, as distinct from superficial, landowner contact with the eduction of rural labourers.

As with schools, so perhaps with churches, closely linked as they were as the centres of authority and social discipline in village life. Unfortunately there are no sources which permit a ready assessment of the extent of landowners' activities in church building, extension, and restoration, let alone of their involvement in the life of the church and the conduct of its parishioners. There were some, like Lord Tollemache at Helmingham in Suffolk, who insisted that all the farmworkers attend church every Sunday; and others like Sir Tatton Sykes who rebuilt or restored twenty churches in the parishes near his seat of Sledmere in the East Riding.[25] It is not likely, however, that such individuals were typical of their class, which by inclination would regard such matters as the parson's business, to attend to as best he could. If concern with succouring and supervising the main agencies which were held to mould the morals and behaviour of the rural labourers was a minority pursuit for landowners, it is possible that concern for their material welfare was more widespread. Next to their wages, which were directly controlled by farmers, not landowners (except for household servants and estate workers), and were effectively determined by the market, housing was the labourers' chief concern. The condition of their home profoundly affected the welfare or misery of a labourer's family; many social observers believed that it was also a decisive influence on their morals. Rural overcrowding was commonly held to encourage immodesty, licentiousness, promiscuity, and incest; a typical view was that 'in the villages where the cottages are most crowded there are the greatest number of illegitimate children'.[26] While overcrowding was also thought to cause intemperance, by driving men to the beer-shops, the drive for cottage improvement was no doubt more strongly nourished by the desire to eradicate incest and promiscuity, an object to be attained by providing enough rooms to separate the sleeping arrangements of the sexes. Success in such endeavours was probably never very great, since the incest taboo seems to have been as firmly held by the labouring as by other classes, and despite the prurient shock with which country parsons and doctors claim to have observed incest it is unlikely ever to have been anything but exceptional; while there are no grounds for supposing that rural fornication fell out of favour.

Even if the desired effects on sexual behaviour may not have been realized, cottages were none the less built. Among a certain group of landowners discussion of cottage improvements and the merits of two- or three-bedroom designs, and the exchange of restrained complaints about the meagre financial returns on cottage building as an investment, became as absorbing as the talk of record bags or record runs among other groups. Many individuals, from Lord Shaftesbury in Dorset – who in spite of his initial confession on inheriting the estate that

> surely I am the most perplexed of men, I have passed my life in rating others for allowing rotten houses and immoral, unhealthy dwellings; and now I come into an estate rife with abominations! Why, there are things here to make one's flesh creep; and I have not a farthing to set them right,

in the end managed to find the money to build many cottages[27] – to the Duke of Northumberland in his county, from the Earl of Leicester in Norfolk to Lord Dartmouth in Staffordshire, acquired considerable reputations in the middle years of the century as builders of model cottages. Some, like the Earl of Leicester, went further, and as well as building cottages, let them direct to the labourers instead of following the normal system of letting cottages along with farms to tenant farmers, who might then use their power to threaten eviction from tied cottages to intimidate their workers; the earl's arrangement turned cottage owning to paternalist account by interposing the landowner as the labourer's protector in this sector of the conflict between farmer and labourer, although it may not have done much to help agricultural efficiency. Individual instances, however, are an unsatisfactory foundation for any generalization; if it is accepted that, by 1914, landowners as a group had built some 22,000 cottages for farmworkers, cottage building is revealed decidedly as a minority pursuit.[28] Several individuals are known to have built 200 or more cottages on their estates in the period of greatest activity, between 1850 and 1880, so that the total may have represented the work of no more than 100–200 landowners. In any case, even in relation to an agricultural work-force which had shrunk by about one third between 1851 and 1911, these cottages cannot have contributed as much as 5 per cent of its housing; it was a rare and untypical labourer's family that experienced the joys of living in a model cottage, or whose home harboured reminders of land-owner influence.

With landowner attention to basic living conditions confined to such a limited scale it is hardly likely that their provision of such frills in the way of village amenities as reading rooms, village halls, or playing fields was more lavish or widespread. Some individual landowners did indeed pro-vide some or all of these things as part of their concept of social duty and leadership, although the impression conveyed by country house literature is that gentry-sponsored sport for the locals was confined to an annual cricket match between the big house eleven and the servants and labour-ers, played on a pitch in the park, until in the early twentieth century the idea of more permanent and specialized playing fields began, especially under the influence of football, to be imported into the countryside from the towns.[29] An even more casual impression is that the great majority of villages went without any public meeting places until the crop of memorial halls began to appear after 1918. It may be that the less expensive and less capital-intensive forms of helping the local community – running a village clothing club, distributing blankets and coal, opening a soup kitchen in winter, subscribing to a local benevolent or friendly society – were more widely practised by landowners. Such help for the needy and encourage-ment to the thrifty, whatever the explicit, conscious motive for giving it, no doubt helped to establish the character, influence, and authority of the donor and thus to preserve his position at the head of the social hierarchy in his country; one might expect it to be given above all to the villages which stood directly outside the park gates, living in the shadow of a big house.

It might seem, indeed, as if all the evidence of landowners' involvement in providing the material equipment of village life – schools, churches, cottages, and clubs – pointed towards the conclusion that their horizons of social responsibility and spheres of active social leadership and control were limited to the villages and parishes that they held in sole ownership. Such an explanation would dovetail neatly with the strong mid-century concern over the distinction between open and close parishes and the differences in their states of misery or well-being. Open parishes were those with no dominant landowner, in which property ownership was diffuse and sites for cottages could be readily acquired; they were over-crowded, overpopulated, poorly housed, heavily burdened with poor rates, and they provided much of the labour, which commuted daily on

95

foot, for working the farms of the close parishes. These, by contrast, were in single ownership, or at most in the hands of two or three owners; the numbers of cottages were carefully controlled and restricted in order to keep population below the labour needs of the parish and thus ensure that poor rates were kept low. It would not be unreasonable to expect that close parishes were the ones to receive close attention. The object of close parishes was to keep down expenditure on the poor, however, and this could be achieved by simple restriction of numbers without any need for the restricted number of cottages to be better than those elsewhere, or for the inhabitants to be better looked after. It could be argued, indeed, that from the point of view of a landowner concerned only with the essential requirements of keeping social order and preserving deference that the powers of property were so complete and unchallengeable in close parishes by virtue of their monopolization, that there was less need than in other places for deploying the more subtle instruments of control through benevolence. Hypotheses aside, the available figures do not support the idea of an association between close parishes and paternalism. In the country as a whole close parishes amounted to perhaps 20 per cent of the total in rural areas at the middle of the century, a proportion much in excess of those which saw any cottage building by landowners. The regional variations in 'closeness', moreover, which range from high points of 33 to 43 per cent of all townships being close in Norfolk, Leicestershire, Rutland, Lincolnshire, and the East Riding, to low points of 6 per cent in Essex, Cambridgeshire, and Hertfordshire, with much of the midland shires and west country in the middle of this range, do not correspond at all with the variations in the support of village schools, unless they hint vaguely at an inverse correlation.[30] There were too many close parishes in the wrong places, for these to have been necessarily the places where village life was most dominated, regulated, nursed, and cosseted by a powerful landowner.

That there were many villages in which there was much doffing of caps, either because people did not dare risk giving offence by doing otherwise or because they wished to show appreciation of favours and good works received, is not in doubt. If the distribution of good works, embodied in churches, schools, cottages, clothing clubs, free coal, soup kitchens, and towards the end of the century, patronage of healthy recreations and the occasional cottage hospital, was not determined by a random scatter of individual landowners and their wives who happened to have lively social consciences, it may well have depended on the residential habits of land-owners and the extent to which particular big houses were identified with immediately dependent villages. A map of rural communities which were particularly under the eye, or thumb, of a landowner patron might well, therefore, be very similar to a map of estate villages, defined as those which, although not necessarily custom-built in uniform style, adorned and complemented the big house and housed estate workers, pensioned dependants, and some of the outdoor servants as well as the more typical village population of farm labourers, village workers, and tradesmen. The map would have many large blank areas, for all the general evidence indicates that paternalism was restricted and localized in its appearances, and above all that it was not systematically deployed in those places and situations where the traditional social order and respect for the law were most threatened by social stresses and strains. It is possible to conclude either that the benefits and comforts of social services provided by land-owners were reserved for a privileged minority in the countryside, or that only a minority were unlucky enough to be subjected to the constraints of social discipline and control imposed from above; either that the majority of landowners neglected their social responsibilities towards the majority of the people living on their estates, because they were indiffer-ent, lazy, or self-centred, or that the majority declined to abuse the power of property by interfering in other people's lives. Either way, for most country folk landowners were remote figures who left them to fend for themselves, living their own lives and fighting their own battles with farmers and other employers. Pockets of sheltered, protected, and regi-mented rural communities studded a landscape populated by much more independent, self-reliant, and exposed villages; which set of communities were more contented, or more resentful of their lot, is an open question.

Notes

1   E. P. Thompson, 1965, ch. 7; Green, 1913.
2   Arch, 1898, 55.
3   Dunbabin, 1974, 14.
4   Howitt, 1838, I, 286, quoted in Horn, 1976b, 5.
5   BPP 1873 XIII, Q. 3028–30.
6   1911 Census, England and Wales, occupation tables, rural districts.
7   BPP 1862 XLV.
8   BPP 1873 XIII, Q. 8067.
9   Arch, 1898, 159.
10 The chief constable thought there were 300 men in Hertfordshire who maintained themselves for several months each year by commercial poaching: BPP 1873 XIII, Q. 240.
11 BPP 1873 XIII, Q. 1616–27, 6653.
12 ibid., Q. 6637.
13 Statistical information is from the occupation tables of the 1861 and 1911 censuses.
14 Itzkowitz, 1977, 146–50.
15 Sources as far apart as Engels, 1950, 266, and the chief constables in Memorial, BPP 1862 XLV 2, agree, approvingly and disapprovingly, that poachers were generally regarded as 'village heroes'. See also Samuel, 1975a, 207–27.
16 *Victoria County History: Lincolnshire I*, 1906, 494; Itzkowitz, 1977, 172–3.
17 BPP 1862 XLV.

18 The figures were 19 police per 10,000 inhabitants in Norfolk, 15 in Leicestershire.
19 The normal ratio in 1911 was 11–12 police per 10,000 inhabitants in the agricultural counties; in Cornwall, Rutland, and Shropshire it was 7–8, and in Hertfordshire, Kent and Surrey 19–21.
20 Hurt, 1971, 22.
21 Hurt, 1968, 6.
22 BPP 1889 LIX, 6–7.
23 BPP 1861 XXI, II 157, 74; I 78.
24 *Victoria County History: Essex VI; Gloucestershire XI; Middlesex V; Oxfordshire VIII, IX, X; Wiltshire X.* A complete count of the National schools mentioned in these volumes shows that the sites were provided, or the costs of building largely met, by

Members of landed aristocracy or gentry	21
Wealthy non-landowners	15
Local clergy	10
Oxford colleges, and bishops	4
No particular individuals	68
Total	118

25 Evans, 1970, 123–4; Pevsner, 1972, 43.
26 Quoted in Burnett, 1978, 45.
27 Hodder, 1887, 449.
28 Whetham, 1978, 48.
29 Girouard, 1978, 271, 285.
30 Holderness, 1972, especially 135.

7

Labour organizations

Pamela Horn

Labour organizations in the Victorian countryside fell into two broad categories. First of all, there were the friendly societies, which had as their principal aim the provision of financial and medical help to members during sickness and old age as well as benefits to cover funeral expenses at death. Secondly, there were the trade unions, whose objective was the more dynamic one of raising general living standards by improving wage rates and reducing the hours of work. Each had its own particular role to play in the lives of country workers.

The history of friendly societies is a long one, dating back in the view of some writers to the craft gilds and religious fraternities which protected skilled workers in the Middle Ages. Certainly, by the late seventeenth century there are accounts of friendly societies which would have been recognizable as such to a nineteenth-century club member.[1] But it was from the middle of the eighteenth century that their numbers began to rise sharply – as with the Beaminster society in Dorset which was formed in May 1762 for 'Parishioners under 30 years of age.' Members were to pay a 3s. entrance fee and a contribution of 2d. per week towards a sick benefit scheme, while meetings were to be held every six weeks on a Monday evening at a local public house. Fines were imposed on those who disrupted proceedings by swearing, coming into the club-room intoxicated with liquor, causing a quarrel and other similar offences. In return, benefits ranging from 4s. to 6s. per week were to be paid during sickness together with a funeral benefit of £3 and a pension of 2s. per week for members aged between 63 and 70, increasing to 2s. 6d. per week for those aged 70 and above. An annual dinner or feast was also to be held, preceded by a procession of members walking 'two by two' to Beaminster church, where a 'sermon [was to] be preached by the Vicar or Curate of the parish'. Any members who failed to take part in the procession 'regularly in their proper places' would be fined the substantial sum of sixpence. In aims and organizations this society was similar to countless fellows in other rural communities during the eighteenth and nineteenth centuries. Indeed, the Beaminster society itself survived in substantially unchanged form until its dissolution in 1892.[2]

But it was following the passage of the 1834 Poor Law Amendment Act that the friendly societies became most popular, as small craftsmen and labourers, anxious to avoid the harshness and stigma of poor relief, made what provision they could to help one another in times of sickness, accident, or death. One of the poor expressed a widespread attitude in declaring: 'We must look out for ourselves, and provide for a day of sickness and old age, now that there is no parish to look to.'[3] And the club banner at Bledington in Gloucestershire expressed the common sentiment with its device of clasped hands and its slogan: 'Bear ye one another's burdens.'[4]

In the early days many of these clubs, like the Beaminster and Bledington societies, were purely local affairs, based upon a single village or town, and often with little financial stability since scant attention was paid to actuarial principles when their rules were formulated. Membership was generally too limited to permit them to meet any unexpectedly heavy drain upon resources, so that 'an epidemic or the bankruptcy of a farmer' might ruin some of the smaller bodies. Other critics felt that rather than being instruments for the encouragement of prudence and thrift, they were often merely an excuse for convivial meetings and for the holding of an annual feast – which might in itself almost exhaust their reserves when it was a substantial dinner washed down by large quantities of beer. In fact, as one witness to the Royal Commission on Friendly Societies sourly remarked in the early 1870s, a number of men merely joined a club because 'it had the best feast and the pleasantest meetings every month'.[5] Its financial strength and stability were little considered.

A further weakness was that in the early years many of the smaller organizations were established on the 'dividing' principle, so that every five or seven years there was a share-out of funds, and then the whole process would start again. Under this arrangement a man 'might find that he was not eligible for re-election because of age or health, and so found himself without assistance when he most needed it'.[6] However, by the middle of the nineteenth century some of these problems were being overcome as the larger and more secure national societies, like the Oddfellows and the Foresters, became increasingly common in country districts. In Dorset, for example, the number of lodges attached to the Manchester Unity of Oddfellows had increased from three in 1845 to thirty-one by 1875, and in Norfolk from forty-eight to ninety-six over the same period.[7] In addition, the Friendly Societies Act of 1875, by encouraging the registration of the smaller societies and by tightening up their financial administration, helped to foster a more responsible attitude to management in the final quarter of the nineteenth century.

Certainly both landowners and farmers encouraged their workers to join benefit clubs by offering prizes at the annual agricultural shows to those men who had been members longest. In some villages, indeed, the local gentry would subscribe towards a society's working expenses – as they did to the clothing and coal clubs which likewise flourished in many communities. (A survey of south Warwickshire parishes in 1893 revealed between twenty and thirty clothing and coal clubs, together with twenty-four pig insurance societies and, in one village, a cow insurance society.)[8] It was felt that the thrifty man would be a more careful worker – and also one less likely to be a burden on the poor rates. Typical of the provision made, therefore, was that of the Loughborough Agricultural Association, which in September 1871 gave a prize of £2 to Joseph Bramley of Kingston, who had been a friendly society member for fifty-six years.[9]

Friendly societies were one way in which men could learn to work together and run their own affairs, while on club nights they had the opportunity to discuss topics of common interest. Both of these aspects were to be of importance when the time came for the formation of agricultural trade unions. Unlike workers in many other industries, farm labourers came relatively late to the idea of unionism. Admittedly the first unsuccessful attempts at combination had been made in the 1830s – the 'Tolpuddle Martyrs' of Dorset in 1833–4 is one obvious example that springs to mind. But their impact was both restricted in scale and short-lived. It was not until the late 1860s, at a time of rising prices and of agitation among urban workers for the 1867 Reform Bill to extend the parliamentary franchise, that sustained interest in unionism began to appear in the rural areas. Among the counties affected at this time was Buckinghamshire, where a Buckingham Farm Labourers' Union was formed in the small parish of Gawcott in the spring of 1867. In a handbill issued in March of that year the men appealed for a wage of 12s. per week, so that they might live 'not as paupers, but by our own industry'.[10] In their efforts to secure higher wages they had a measure of success. But in terms of leadership and in area of recruitment the union was too limited to make any lasting impression.

Other attempts at combination were also made at around this time, so that in 1866 an ephemeral Agricultural Labourers' Protection Association was established in Kent, with a similar body set up in the following year in the vicinity of Leicester. However, it was not until 1871 that a more permanent organization was at last established, centred upon the counties of Shropshire and Herefordshire and operating under the name of the North Herefordshire and South Shropshire Agricultural Labourers' Improvement Society. It was an essentially peaceful organization, with the slogan 'Emigration, Migration, but not Strikes'. At its peak it claimed a membership of about 30,000 in six different counties, and one of its main achievements was the dispatching of 'surplus' labour from low-wage Herefordshire to better-paid employment in Yorkshire, Lancashire, and Staffordshire.

In the months that followed, similar organizations appeared in Leicestershire and Lincolnshire, the latter under the leadership of a local republican agitator named William Banks.[11] Each had as its principal objective the improvement of wage rates at a time of sharply increasing prices and of general trade boom. Yet, despite these pioneering ventures, it was from agitation among the labourers of south Warwickshire that the prime inspiration of the rural union movement was to derive. The Warwickshire men began to combine in February 1872 under the leadership of Joseph Arch, a 45-year-old hedgecutter from the village of Barford and a Primitive Methodist local preacher. Arch was a man of great determination, and as he stumped the countryside addressing meetings during the wet spring of 1872 he was able to instil some of his steely qualities into his listeners. For, as he subsequently wrote: 'All that stirring time I felt as if there was a living fire in me. It seemed to me that I was fulfilling a mission; that I had been raised up for the work . . . The people responded nobly to the call.'[12] Many of the union songs of those days paid tribute to his role – as in the chorus of 'We'll All Be Union Men':

> Joe Arch he raised his voice,
> 'Twas for the working man,
> Then let us all rejoice and say,
> We'll all be Union men.[13]

The timing of this upsurge of militancy is significant, for it came at the end of a period of prosperity for English agriculture – albeit a prosperity in which the farm-worker had shared to but a limited degree. At the same time the passage of the 1871 Trade Union Act had drawn attention to the legal and financial benefits which unions could now enjoy, while the success of a contemporary movement for a nine-hour working day among engineers and builders further underlined the possible benefits of combination. It is notable that one of the early demands of the agricultural unions was for a nine-hour day, though this was later dropped when the main attention of the men turned to securing higher wages and an end to the truck system in wage payments.[14] By the early 1870s the isolation and ignorance of rural labourers were gradually being eroded. Thanks to the availability of railway excursions, increased elementary school provision, cheaper newspapers, and the activities of emigration agents, their knowledge of the outside world and its prospects was steadily increasing.

Once the Warwickshire men had formed their union they were anxious to achieve positive benefits from it as quickly as possible. So, early in March 1872, they put forward demands for an increase in wages to 2s. 8d. a day and a reduction in the hours of work. These proposals were incorporated in a circular letter which was sent to local farmers in the Wellesbourne area. The latter ignored the missive, believing that the new organization would prove too weak to support effective industrial action. But on 11 March their complacency was rudely shattered when the men came out on strike.[15]

Press publicity followed rapidly, and from an early stage money began to flow into the union's coffers, sent by a sympathetic general public anxious to help provide strike benefit – for most of the men were too poor to have resources of their own to fall back upon. A number moved to better-paid employment elsewhere in England, while a few emigrated to New Zealand and, less happily, to Brazil. But most stayed in their home community and were eventually rewarded with an increase in pay. The dispute was finally wound up in the middle of April, but its effect in rousing rural workers in other parts of the country was a good deal more permanent. As the *Eastern Morning News and Hull Advertiser* of 8 April 1872 put it:

> Two years ago a strike of agricultural labourers would have been deemed impossible. It was believed that our clod hoppers were incapable of combination. Yet, now that a combination has been effected, that a strike has been struck, the movement is spreading over the country with marvellous rapidity.[16]

In the meantime, on 29 March at a large demonstration held at Leamington, the new Warwickshire Agricultural Labourers' Union was formally established under the leadership of Joseph Arch. Two months later this body was to form the nucleus of the National Agricultural Labourers' Union, the first national society ever to cater for farmworkers. By now Arch's fame had spread throughout the countryside, and although not all of the local unions which sprang up in these hectic weeks joined the NALU – the Lincolnshire Labour League and the Kent and Sussex Union were two which stayed out – there were representatives from most of the counties in southern and central England among the sixty or so delegates who attended its inauguration at Leamington. Their speeches were punctuated with 'devout utterances of "Amen", and "Praise Him" ', for many of the most active leaders of the new organization were, like Arch himself, local Methodist preachers. Indeed, in the three counties of Lincolnshire, Norfolk, and Suffolk alone, 95 per cent of the leaders whose religious affiliations can be traced were Methodists of one kind or another.[17] And in many respects the forms of meeting adopted by the union were adaptations of Primitive Methodist practice: 'Social, missionary, and fundraising elements were characteristic of the tea meetings held by both organizations. Premises and equipment were lent between the two.'[18]

There was more than a hint of millenarianism, too, in some of the speeches made at this first gathering. As one delegate declared: 'Sir, this be a blessed day: this 'ere Union be the Moses to lead us poor men up out o' Egypt.' While another man, deliberating on the ways of Divine Providence, declared that 'he were remoinded o' many things in th' Scripters, more perticler o' th' ram's horns what blew down th' walls o' Jericho, and frightened Pharaoh, King of Egypt'.[19]

Once the preliminary arrangements had been completed, Arch was unanimously elected president of the National Union. In the following month a sympathetic Leamington newspaper owner and journalist, J. E. Matthew Vincent, who had agreed to act as union treasurer, also helped it to launch a newspaper, the *Labourers' Union Chronicle*. This latter was to provide a valuable link for the movement, since in its pages could be found reports of branch and district assemblies from all over the country, as well as general discussions of union policy. Within two years it could boast a circulation of over 50,000, and it is significant that both the Kent and Sussex Union and the Lincolnshire Labour League also had newspapers of their own from an early stage.

In the months that followed the formation of the NALU the pressure for higher wages continued. But one of the major weaknesses of the movement was that it never managed to recruit a majority of farmworkers. Even at its peak in the spring of 1874, when there were around 86,200 NALU members, plus perhaps a further 49,000 belonging to other independent organizations like the Lincolnshire Labour League, this was still a small minority of the one million or so male and female agricultural labourers, shepherds, and farm servants employed in England and Wales.[20] Even in the best unionized counties the NALU was unable to recruit more than about one in three or one in four of the men. In part this was due to the nature of agricultural employment itself, with small groups of workers in isolated units having little opportunity to meet together to discuss their grievances. Then, too, many of them lived in tied cottages and faced the possibility not only of dismissal but of eviction from their homes if they offended their employers by being overactive in the wrong cause.[21] None the less, despite these difficulties considerable progress was made. In many areas, indeed, pay advances were won without resort to strike action.[22] But farmers and landowners much resented this intervention by 'outsiders' in rural labour relations – and it was a development they were determined to resist. The Earl of Denbigh, for example, warned his workers against 'paid agitators, who are going about deceiving the people as to their true and highest interests', and he threatened to evict from their cottages any who refused to work when 'fair wages and conditions' were offered to them by the farmers; Joseph Arch himself was denounced as an 'agitator, an apostle of arson, who was setting class against class'.[23]

It was against this background that in the spring of 1874 the NALU faced its stiffest challenge in the eastern counties – one of the best organized areas in the country – from agriculturists determined to end once and for all the 'dictatorship' of its officials in wage matters. The immediate cause of the dispute was a demand during February 1874 by labourers in the small Suffolk village of Exning for a rise of 1s. a week. Their employers, who had joined together in the Newmarket Farmers' Defence Association, responded by locking out all union men on their books. In this unplanned, almost casual, fashion, therefore, the dispute began. In the months that followed it spread to many of the surrounding counties, with nineteen different union districts eventually involved.[24] Ultimately about 6,000 men were drawn into the conflict, and the National Union executive committee was involved in paying strike benefits amounting to over £24,000. Once the dispute was under way one of the major tasks for Arch and his fellow leaders was to try to raise funds to support the men locked out. But the scale of operation proved too great for them and on 27 July it was decided to recommend those men still out to return to work. In the event some found difficulty in doing so, and although a number emigrated, others were re-employed only on the understanding that they left the union.[25]

Although the outcome was probably inevitable, given the financial fragility of the NALU and the scale of expenditure required to support the men in dispute, there is no doubt that the July surrender led to disillusion among many members. From this there developed conflicts among the union leaders themselves, so that in the spring of 1875 J. E. Matthew Vincent, the NALU treasurer, broke away to form a new, though short-lived, body called the National Farm Labourers' Union. This had as its main objectives the provision of allotments and smallholdings, and the avoidance of strikes. In the months that followed its leaders and those of the NALU indulged in bitter recriminations, in which the small independent unions which had survived also joined. Naturally this did little to encourage their supporters, especially at a time when the movement was already under pressure from a serious decline in arable farming following bad harvests at home and growing imports of cheap grain from abroad. NALU membership slumped to a mere 20,000 by 1880, as the union proved unable to withstand 'the economic pressure from without, and the fierce dissensions from within'.[26] Three years earlier, in a desperate attempt to strengthen the loyalty of members, it had embarked on a sick benefit scheme; but sadly, as with many similar bodies outside its ranks, this had served rather to weaken its financial structure than to strengthen it, as withdrawals soon began to exceed payments. In that respect the Kent and Sussex Union had a rather more successful career, with the arrangement of voluntary 'good feeling' collections from an early stage to cover sickness, bereavement, emigration expenses, and similar matters. Eventually, in the autumn of 1874, the union decided to establish a permanent sick fund of its own.[27]

By the early 1880s, then, due to the general economic difficulties, wage rates were beginning to fall back from the peaks achieved in the upsurge of 1872–4 as employers reacted to the drop in food prices by cutting labour bills. Paradoxically, the cheapening of foodstuffs did mean that, despite their smaller cash earnings, the real incomes of most labourers rose in the 1880s. Even cash payments did not fall to pre–1872 levels. Nevertheless, the fact that unions could give so little protection in the vital matter of wages served to add to the disillusion of their members.

By this time a number of the remaining unionists were turning away from purely economic concerns to the political field, pressing for a widening of the franchise to rural workers to match the rights given to townsmen in 1867. Even in the early days franchise reform had been a feature of NALU policy, with the *Labourers' Union Chronicle* putting the acquisition of the vote second only to higher wages as a union objective as early as June 1873. Although in the final pressure for reform in 1884 the union's influence was weakened by losses of membership – with support for the NALU down to a mere 15,000 by the end of 1883 – Arch, at any rate, did not allow himself to be downcast. During the exciting months as the Bill passed through Parliament he addressed many village meetings on the issue, speaking from a Liberal standpoint – he had long been a strong supporter of the Radical wing of that party.

Rural householders were admitted to full political rights in December 1884, and at the general election held in the following year Arch was elected Liberal member for the North-West Norfolk constituency. His success was indicative of results in other rural areas where Liberal gains were also recorded. Unfortunately from his point of view, the shadow of Irish Home Rule hung over the new Parliament from the beginning, and when the Liberal Party split over the issue in the early summer of 1886 Arch was among the pro-Home Rule supporters of Gladstone who lost their seats at the general election held shortly after. For him and for the union the next years were bleak ones. In the face of agricultural depression and dwindling support there was little that could be achieved, and by 1889 NALU membership had slumped to a mere 4,254, while that of the Lincolnshire Labour League had dropped to only 90, as compared with the 18,000 or so it had claimed in 1873.[28] The Kent and Sussex Union had by this time become involved with the recruitment of general labourers rather than solely with those working on the farms, and in 1892 it changed its name to the London and Counties Labour League and moved its headquarters to London.

However, just as the demise of the whole movement seemed imminent, an upsurge of trade, coupled with the successful outcome of a strike by London dockers, gave a brief reprieve. Poorly paid workers in a whole variety of industries – including agriculture – were inspired to combine once more. The NALU shared in this revival, particularly in Norfolk, where it had to thank the tireless efforts of the local organizer, Zacharias Walker, also an active Primitive Methodist lay preacher. Here a membership of over 12,000 was recorded in 1891, and in the general election held in the following year Arch recovered his seat as Liberal member for North-West Norfolk – a position he continued to occupy until his retirement from public life in 1900.[29]

The NALU was not the only body to benefit from this change of fortune. Even the Lincolnshire Labour League pushed up its membership to almost 300 by 1890. But, more significantly, a Radical organization called the English Land Restoration League, set up in 1884 to promote land-tax reform, now sought to win farm labourers to its cause by supporting a number of county agricultural unions. It also aimed to improve wages and housing conditions in rural areas. Even the London Dockers' Union, concerned at the ability of farmworkers to migrate to the capital and undercut the wages of its members, recruited briefly among the rural labourers in Oxfordshire and Lincolnshire in the early 1890s.[30] But it was the Land Restoration League which was the more effective of these two bodies. Its first 'missionary' tour was organized in 1891 in Suffolk, where its representatives worked alongside the newly established Eastern Counties Labour Federation, whose headquarters were at Ipswich. The campaign was a success and was quickly followed by others, with county unions springing up in Norfolk, Wiltshire, Berkshire, Hertfordshire, Hereford-shire, and Warwickshire. But apart from the Eastern Counties Labour Federation, which in 1892 claimed a membership of almost 17,000, the new organizations had little success. In some cases their Radical leadership, and the fact that farm labourers were not prominent on their executives, may have contributed to this failure. Thus the Berkshire Union was financed largely by two middle-class Socialist sisters from the small town of Wok-ingham.[31] Perhaps not surprisingly in view of its financial weakness the rule book of this latter society carefully stated in 1892: 'Our members are requested to observe that they must not go on strike without the written authority of the Executive Committee, as we are anxious to avoid strikes in all cases if possible. Arbitration is more efficient than strikes.'[32] At that stage the union had a membership of about 570 out of a total agricultural work force in Berkshire at this time of over 17,000, including both male and female labourers.

Everywhere, in fact, the rural revival proved short-lived, for the early 1890s saw a fresh onset of general economic recession and, in rural areas, the serious effects of drought upon crop yields. Arable farmers were hit by the continuing importation of cheap foreign grain – in 1894 wheat prices reached their lowest level for the century – and meat and dairy producers were facing increased competition from abroad. Inevitably the bargaining position of the unions weakened, and one by one they collapsed. The NALU itself was wound up in 1896, and in the following year the English Land Restoration League abandoned its rural campaigns. The remnants of the Kent and Sussex Union disappeared in 1895, and although the Lincolnshire Labour League claimed a membership of twenty-one in 1900, it was to all intents and purposes moribund.

Yet, despite this decline, there were some gains to show for this second brief spurt of agitation. Wage rates had been raised for many labourers in the initial upswing, and these gains were largely retained in the years that followed. In addition, when the first parish councils came into being at the end of 1894 labourers in villages where branches of trade unions still survived stood a greater chance of being elected to the new bodies. Thus, of the Norfolk parish elections a contemporary declared: 'The success of the Norfolk labourers [placed] them in the van of the army of labour; they have without doubt achieved a signal victory.' In Warwickshire, ninety-one 'labourers' candidates' were elected with the support of the county agricultural labourers' union, fifty-four of them being farmworkers and the remainder artisans and tradesmen adopted and run by the local branches of the union.[33] Elsewhere labourers were often too diffident to put themselves forward for election against more influential members of village society. And even the limited progress registered in 1894 was not maintained at subsequent contests. None the less, despite their weaknesses, without these union ventures of the 1890s 'a whole generation of labourers would have grown up without experience of combination'.[34]

Perhaps the fairest assessment of the role of agricultural unions in the later nineteenth century has, in fact, been made by Ernest Selley:

Though the Unions did not succeed in permanently improving the labourers's economic position, they gave him a taste of power. He was no longer a submissive, inarticulate beast of burden. His back had been straightened; he stood erect and took his own measure. The Unions had given him knowledge; they had given him a voice . . . In villages where formerly there had been practically no communal life, the Unions had succeeded in drawing the labourers together in social intercourse.[35]

However, not all contemporaries would have agreed with his favourable comments. In particular, the Nonconformist-led unions were accused by many village clergymen of undermining relationships between themselves and their parishioners – as at Chearsley, Buckinghamshire, where the incumbent complained in 1875:

Lately the agents of the NALU have been in the parish, & held meetings, often on Sundays, & they have disquieted the people, & said much against Landowners & the Clergy . . . there can be no doubt that the congregation diminished, & the people became irregular in their attendance, & careless about their public religious duties.[36]

Even when the union movement had faded away, some of the parish clergy's residual suspicion survived to poison relations between the incumbent and his flock over such matters as distribution of village charities and allocation of allotment land. In this regard it is worth noting that when Arch died in February 1919, the *Church Times* declared in an obituary:

> It is regrettable, when we look back to the early days of the agitation he led, to recall the loss of a great opportunity by the country clergy. They might have won the labourers to the Church, but, largely ranging themselves on the side of the squirearchy, they alienated, in too many instances, their struggling parishioners. Since then a more enlightened spirit has prevailed but there remains much leeway to be made up.

Meanwhile, as the days of Arch and the NALU faded, men who were dissatisfied with village life left the land for good, creating fears of 'rural depopulation' in the last years of the nineteenth century.[37] In fostering the spirit of independence which made that migration possible the rural unions undoubtedly played an important role.

Notes

1 Gosden, 1961, 1–2
2 Hine, 1928, 115–20.
3 Russell, 1975, 3.
4 Ashby, 1974, 376.
5 BPP 1872 XXVI Q. 26, 357.
6 Springall, 1936, 60.
7 Gosden, 1961, 31.
8 Ashby and King, 1893, 203.
9 *Loughborough Advertiser*, 5 October 1871.
10 Bucks. RO: Gawcott labourers' handbill; Horn, 1973, 298–301.
11 Dunbabin, 1974, 74.
12 Arch, 1898, 78.
13 Sage, 1951, 20.
14 Horn, 1971, 19, 47.
15 ibid., 49.
16 Russell, n.d., 18; Horn, 1972, 89–92.
17 Scotland, 1977, 4.
18 Gurden, 1976, 5.
19 'Labourers in council', *Congregationalist*, 1872, 421.
20 Horn, 1971, 24, 73.
21 ibid., 52.
22 Horn, 1976b, 132.
23 Sage, 1951, 14; Horn, 1974b, 134.
24 Green, 1920, 56.
25 Horn, 1971, 109–10.
26 Green, 1920, 69.
27 Arnold, 1974, 84–5.
28 Dunbabin, 1974, 80–1.
29 Horn, 1971, 206–10.

30 Horn, 1974a, 19–20.
31 *Reading Observer*, 2 July 1892, 30 June 1894.
32 Rule 30 of the Rules of the Berkshire Agricultural and General Workers' Union: PRO FS 7.18.817.
33 Horn, 1976b, 142–3.
34 Peacock, 1962, 177.
35 Selley, 1919, 80, 82.
36 Bodleian Library, Oxford: MS Oxf. Dioc. Pp. c. 340.
37 Orwin and Whetham, 1964, 332–3.

8

Rural crime and protest in the Victorian era

David Jones

For many years it was customary to ignore the protests of rural labourers which arose between 1830 and 1870, except to contrast their rarity with the frequency of those in town and city. The Chartist movement had little success in the countryside, and trade unionism never established a firm hold there. Crime, too, especially the rising tide of theft and juvenile delinquency in the second quarter of the century, was generally assumed to be an urban problem. Only in the later decades of the twentieth century have scholars begun to look closely at this aspect of the rural scene. They have discovered that, in some areas at least, the spectacular exploits of 'Captain Swing' or 'Rebecca' were part of a continuous pattern of crime and protest. Dr Peacock tells us that the rural labourer in East Anglia 'protested *all* of the time, and most of the time very effectively indeed'.[1] Direct action was one of the few weapons in his armoury.

Contemporaries were not unaware of this situation. Although some landowners in Parliament praised the quiescence of the peasantry at critical moments, their private correspondence in the early Victorian years was often full of uncertainty and alarm. Other observers of rural society could be more detached, and did much to demolish the pleasant myth of the 'innocence and simplicity' of the peasantry. Some of them relished the task. Middle-class reformers like John Bright, Edwin Chadwick, and Thomas Campbell Foster revealed the darker side of village life, as did Thomas Plint and other defenders of the new urban order.[2] Rural workmen, they claimed, were more ignorant, superstitious, immoral, and criminal than their counterparts elsewhere. The last accusation proved highly controversial, partly because so much depended on the districts chosen for comparison. While it was true, for instance, that rural Wales and the north-west had a low recorded level of serious crime in the middle years of the century, commitments for trial in East Anglia were well above the national average. John Glyde, who made a unique regional study of crime at this time, identified Suffolk villages in which violence and malicious damage to property were more common than in large neighbouring towns.[3] At certain periods, as in 1843–4 and 1849–51, such intimidation and destruction of property reached a massive scale, and indicated that paternalism and deference were vitally fractured.

It is difficult to measure the extent and movement of crime and protest during the Victorian years. Many petty session files no longer exist, contemporary opinion could be notoriously unreliable, and newspaper coverage was highly selective. Only after the administrative changes of the late 1850s are we able to calculate the number of crimes known to the police. Even so, all criminal statistics are of limited value. The dark figure of unrecorded crime was undoubtedly important in some rural areas. Judges in Wales in the second half of the century were suspicious of the empty calendars, and policemen there sometimes admitted that violence and petty theft were much greater than most people realized. Farmers were regularly criticized in the early Victorian period for not protecting their property and for not reporting depredations on it. Some of them budgeted for such losses, and in bad years even welcomed the insurance payments for arson. Accusations were also made at this time that farmers sympathized with certain criminals, especially poachers, sometimes letting them off with a warning or a beating. And, finally, many cases were not prosecuted because of the fear of reprisals in the shape of personal violence, animal maiming, and incendiarism. In Cheshire and Suffolk this was one popular contemporary interpretation of the phrase, 'the tyranny of the countryside'.[4]

Changes in the character, numbers, and efficiency of the police also had an effect on the incidence of crime in the countryside. The traditional form of policing was a mixture of community and private enterprise. Although some observers spoke highly of the work of the old village constables, they were a poor organ of social control and in many districts their impact on crime was very limited. They were essentially a part-time defensive force, owing loyalties to their communities, and unable to suppress major outbreaks of crime or disorder, as the events of 1830–44 cruelly demonstrated. The authorities preferred to rely in an emergency on a system of rewards, special constables, and military help. Private policing, too, had long been popular in rural society, with farmers arming their families, employing watchmen to guard their estates, and forming protection societies. Many such associations were established in the south and east during the 1830s, and these paid for professional policemen and met the expenses of prosecuting poachers, sheep-stealers, and the like.

Ironically, the cost of these ventures strengthened the widespread opposition to the establishment of a national police force. By the time the County and Borough Police Act was passed in 1856 only about half the counties had appointed paid policemen. From the beginning the country poor were suspicious of the new police, and their arrival caused protests and riots in many areas. Although there were considerable disputes over the impact of the 'blues' on village life, most seemed to agree that they quickly established themselves as an 'improving agency'. Much to the delight of the clergy, the paid policemen imposed new standards of order in the community. They attended fairs, festivals, and public houses, and gave a new dimension to the term 'Sunday observance'. They also provided greater protection for persons and property. In Hampshire, Essex, and Norfolk families and gangs of sheep stealers and poachers were ruthlessly dispersed. Night patrols and constant harassment kept the 'idle and dissolute' on their guard, and the Poaching Prevention Act of 1862 legalized the hated practice of searching working people on the road. Again, in Dorset, Norfolk, and some other counties the new police were used in somewhat brutal fashion to remove vagrants or gipsies from the countryside. Finally, they helped to ensure the free and safe passage of goods from one region to another. Altogether, then, one can see why many property owners were quickly converted to the benefits of appointing officers, and why problem villages like Wymondham in Norfolk and Hindon near Bradford in Wiltshire were said to have been transformed by their presence. Even so, it is worth remembering that police numbers remained small in some villages, that criminals and vagrants moved to unpoliced areas, and that episodes such as the remarkable Rebecca poaching raids in mid-Wales could reduce them to helplessness.[5]

Another factor affecting the crime rate was changes in prosecution. In the early Victorian period new legislation and the coming of the new police made prosecutions cheaper, commitments more certain, and punishments less severe. The result, much to the chagrin of some contemporaries, was that villagers, especially juveniles, were taken to court for petty theft and minor breaches of the peace that had once been ignored. Much, of course, depended on the initiative of the large property owners. For them, legal prosecutions were only one aspect of the wider question of control and discipline. Landowners who displayed ruthlessness in dealing with the 'Swing' rioters sometimes used mere cautions and confessions during the game law controversy of the 1840s and election disputes of the 1860s. In some areas, too, where work was scarce, social prosecution of criminals through loss of job, home, and income could be just as effective as legal action.[6] Similarly, the wider village community had its own way of dealing with offenders without resort to law. In the more remote parts of Britain the mock trial and physical intimidation were regularly used in the 1830s and 1840s, and were not unknown two generations later.

It is impossible, therefore, to estimate the extent of crime and protest in the countryside. The labourers were a 'secret people' and all we can say with certainty is that the authorities reacted with alarm in the second quarter of the century and with growing confidence thereafter.

Contemporaries attributed much of the tension in rural society to the collapse of mutual respect between classes. The Rev. Henry Worsley of Easton in Suffolk argued in 1849 that crime and protest were the natural result of neglect in a paternalist society.[7] A contrast was drawn between those parts of northern, midland, and western Britain where the concept of a one-class society was grounded in the reality of people working, living, and playing together, and other districts where important proprietors had distanced themselves physically and culturally from the rest of the village community. Flora Thompson was to write later of the 'Romans' and 'Britons' of the countryside, and her metaphor is a useful one.[8] In parts of the south and east two separate worlds faced each other, the one trying to impose its view of the countryside, justice, and history on the other. The Swing riots of 1830 revealed the gulf between rich and poor in the village, but in one sense the protests over the 1834 Poor Law Amendment Act were more significant. For many, this Act was the final confirmation that landowners, farmers, and clergymen placed their own selfish economic interests before those of the wider community. And with alienation came sullenness and a desire for revenge:

> It was a matter of congratulation among the men as they talked at work they had succeeded in 'doing' a person in a better position, or even if they had 'sloped summat' from the well-to-do . . . It is the idea of a legitimate prey, the right to make some folk disgorge, the suggestion of a just reprisal! It is often the same spirit, too, which initiates poaching rather than actual material gain.[9]

Significantly, the major outbreaks of discontent in the years before Arch's union were preceded by sharp increases in rural crime, especially poaching.

Complaints about the commercial and sectional approach of farming people usually revolved around the issues of employer-employee relationships, custom, and charity. During the forty years following the conclusion of the Napoleonic Wars the insecurity of the labourers of the south and east took on new dimensions. Their contracts were shortened or cast aside, allowances or perks of fuel, produce, and grazing were reduced, and wages were kept low by all manner of devices. Under-employment was widespread, not least amongst the young adults, and unemployment, too, was a permanent feature of villages, like Hawkhurst in Kent and Coombs in Suffolk. This situation bred frustration, especially in areas such as northern Essex and the Norfolk-Suffolk border where the population was very dependent on corn production and where alternative employment was scarce and declining. Various surveys of the 1830s and 1840s revealed that riotous protest and arson were most common in districts and periods of poor employment and low wages, that theft fluctuated with the cost of living index, and that poaching and animal stealing increased noticeably once the harvest money had been spent. Threatening letters and outbursts in court told the same story: 'farmers, we are starven, we will not stan this no longer.' The introduction of machinery and the employment of non-parish labour was often the final insult to families on 7s. a week.[10]

Such people were unusually sensitive to changes in customary rights and charity. Proprietors in the Victorian years continued to press their claims to Crown, common, waste, and forest land, and their actions were sometimes bitterly resented by squatters and inhabitants of the 'open villages'.[11] In Oxfordshire, Norfolk and Caernarvonshire, for instance, there were long struggles between 1830 and 1870 over the loss of fuel, grazing, and game.[12] In Wales, and some English districts, many of the crimes of theft, and some of violence, occurred on disputed or newly enclosed land. What caused particular annoyance was the legislation defining ownership of wild produce, birds, fish, and animals. Posters on some south midland farms in the middle of the century warned the poor not to take berries, mushrooms, cress, rabbits, and birds. At the same time, attempts were made to limit customs of gleaning corn, root vegetables, and fallen wood. Relays of old men, women, and children appeared before early Victorian courts pleading their innocence before 'God and tradition'.[13]

Charity was another 'long-established right'. Most villages had received bequests of land, houses, and money for the poor, and there were annual gifts of clothing and fuel. However, certain kinds of charity were being criticized at the very time when they were most needed. Donations were increasingly being given not as of right, but on conditions and in a manner that angered working people. Parish lands in East Anglia were sometimes divided into allotments for the 'better class of labourers' or let out cheaply to farmers, and the income used to finance unpopular poor law policies. The battle over charity land and rights has been much neglected by historians, but it was a recurring theme in the protests, threatening letters, and reminiscences of village folk.[14]

At the heart of this conflict was the question of poor relief. This relief had long been regarded in some districts as a necessary allowance for the lowly paid and the unemployed. Changes in the administration and size of relief had often provoked an angry response, but the New Poor Law produced widespread disbelief.[15] The poor felt, with good reason, that a right had been replaced by a mechanism of control. Farmers who dominated the boards of guardians manipulated the new system to keep wages low, especially for the young, and to remove the 'idle and desperate' from their parishes. As new workhouses were built, stricter regimes introduced, and rates reduced during the late 1830s and early 1840s, labourers vented their anger on the person and property of poor law officials. 'Better go to gaol than starve or go to the union' became the standard excuse of a generation of rural criminals, and the immediate result in some of the southern and eastern counties was a sharp rise in offences both inside and outside the workhouse.[16]

The economic or 'rational' approach to relationships in the countryside was accompanied by an assault on traditional village culture. Once again the targets were the 'idle', 'dissolute', and 'desperate', and the objectives were control, respectability, and productivity. The attack, which came from both outside and inside the village, was conducted through the church, the school, and the law. The years between 1830 and 1870 saw the disappearance of many holidays, fairs, and 'violent and sensual' amusements, and the emergence, in certain parts of Britain, of an alternative recreational pattern. Where popular protests were unavailing, many of the labourers signalled their indifference to the march of progress by their persistent attendance at the beerhouse. Beerhouses, which were legalized by an Act of 1830, were condemned by many observers as the home of rural crime; and there were indeed famous drinking places like the Chequers Inn, Thetford (Norfolk), and Higg's beerhouse in Charlton (Oxfordshire) in which poaching and protests were organized. Ministers, policemen, and a new breed of temperance reformers launched several major onslaughts against the village pub and produced a series of waves in the crime statistics.[17]

Law, then, was used in the nineteenth century as in the eighteenth, to push through radical changes in relation to property, custom, charity, and behaviour. The peasantry reacted to these changes in various ways; in mid-Wales emigration was a traditional response; in parts of the south-west there were reports of deep fatalism amongst the poorest labourers, while in East Anglia hostility tended to remain near the surface. Certain villages, like the large open communities, seemed especially prone to crime and protest, though much depended on local circumstances. Paternalistic regimes and individual acts of kindness help to explain why places like Langley in Essex remained extraordinarily stable in a sea of discontent. After brief periods of resistance many villages settled down to enjoy a kind of peace in the mid-Victorian years, but others, such as Exning in Suffolk, had an inextinguishable militancy.[18]

A study of crime statistics reveals that the countryside, like Britain generally, experienced a marked rise in the number of offences during the first half of the century, with the highest peak in the early 1840s.[19] The crime rate remained high until the early 1850s and then fell persistently, despite brief recoveries, as in the late 1860s and early 1880s. Within this overall trend, however, there were some interesting developments.[20] Crimes of violence, which formed between one-tenth and one-fifth of rural offences, continued to worry the authorities until the critical turning-point of the mid-1860s. Typical cases were family and neighbour disputes, drunken brawls, and the Sunday pranks of young servants. In the early 1830s and early 1840s the incidence of serious assault reached record levels, and there were reports from East Anglia, Somerset, and Cheshire of 'respectable' people being unable to leave their homes after dark for fear of being attacked and robbed.[21] The people who suffered most were farmers, agents, gamekeepers, poor law officials, and policemen. At least twenty keepers were murdered in the years 1843 and 1844, and in Staffordshire alone double that number were injured in fights during the sixteen months September 1860 to January 1862.[22] The new police were also frequently assaulted on their first appearance in the countryside, as the statistics of the late 1850s and early 1860s indicate. Some of these victims were shot and maimed in the most brutal fashion.

The major crime in the countryside was undoubtedly theft, though one notes a significant decline in reported cases during the second half of Victoria's reign. Earlier, incidents of stealing were very common in difficult years like 1837, 1842 and 1868, and many of them occurred in the winter months. The most notorious form of theft was of farm produce and livestock. Wood, corn, vegetables, fruit, and cheese were taken from sheds, barns, fields, allotments, and gardens, usually by labourers and their families. The loss of poultry, sheep, cattle, and horses was a more serious affair, and was at its height in the late 1830s and early 1840s, although in the south-west it was still a prime concern ten years later, and in Cumberland forty years later. In the less-policed parts of Lincolnshire, Norfolk, and Essex the daily losses were so enormous that weary farmers guarded their herds day and night.[23] Finally, the theft of rabbits, hares, gamebirds, and fish sometimes reached astonishing proportions. In 1843, for instance, one in four convictions in Suffolk was against the game laws, while in Norfolk over 2,000 poachers were fined or imprisoned in the years 1863–71.[24] Many of the poachers were young labourers who took a few rabbits at weekends, but there were also – as in the case of sheep stealing – gangs based in villages and towns. These gangs, often armed and disguised, may have virtually controlled isolated parts of the countryside before the Poaching Prevention Act in 1862.[25]

Crimes of trespass and malicious damage formed a small but persistent element in the statistics of rural crime. Unfortunately, it is difficult to distinguish between ordinary criminal offences and those which are regarded as acts of protest. The removal of gates and fences, which so annoyed East Anglian farmers in the first half of the century, was both a common youthful prank and a recognized form of intimidation and revenge. Similarly, prosecutions for trespass and for the destruction of weirs, walls, trees, and produce could indicate battles over disputed property and rights of way. The bitter conflict between Welsh landowners and squatters in the later years of Victoria's reign has not yet been researched.[26] The most serious of this category of crimes was arson, and we know that most cases were the result of pique and protest. Rural incendiarism reached unprecedented levels in the period between the Swing riots and the emergence of Arch's union. During the outbreaks of 1843–4, 1849–52, 1862–4, and 1868–9, burning ricks and outhouses were often a daily fact of life for farmers south of a line from the Wash to the Severn, and fires continued to flare in Hampshire, Dorset, and certain other counties during later years of tension.[27] In the 1860s, however, there was a change in the character of this crime: an increasing number of these offences were carried out by vagrants. In north Wales during this decade at least forty-nine of the eighty-two people charged with arson at the assizes can be identified as tramps.[28]

Other important groups of rural crime included poor law and vagrancy offences. These were committed by the 'lowest' members of society and reflected economic influences and the initiatives of government and local authorities. A small but constant stream of labourers appeared before the courts charged with deserting or neglecting to support their families, and a more irregular number were found guilty of misconduct in the work-house. The latter crime, which involved tearing clothes, smashing windows, refusal to work, arson, and riot, was especially prominent in the 1830s and 1840s, and again in the late 1860s and early 1870s. During these times, south-west Wales, Norfolk and Suffolk, and parts of the western and home counties, witnessed something of an institutional revolt.[29] Vagrancy offences were also a matter of deep anxiety in these years. In counties such as Cumberland, Merioneth, Kent, and Shropshire tramps and gipsies were blamed for almost all petty crime in the countryside. The problem of vagrants was never solved but rather, as the statistics and conferences at the turn of the century demonstrated, simply pushed from one district to the next.[30]

Although vagrancy and certain other offences remained a permanent source of concern in the second half of the nineteenth century, there were, nevertheless, important changes in the composition of rural crime during this period. Cases of assault and stealing, which had once constituted about a half of all petty session proceedings, lost much of their prominence in the criminal statistics. Their place was partly taken by newer categories of crime. In the 1880s and 1890s as many as a quarter of all offences involved cruelty to animals and breaches of the Education and Highways Acts. Villagers still continued to be arrested in large numbers for drunkenness and disorderly conduct, but the high figures of the 1870s and 1880s may well indicate changes in prosecution policy as much as a frightening outburst of debauchery.[31]

By the close of the Victorian era there can be little doubt that the alarming violence which had characterized the 1830s and 1840s had largely evaporated. Reports and reminiscences of the turn of the century tell of village constables who spent much of their time on routine matters, keeping an eye out for vagrants and poachers, and grumbling when called upon to apprehend mere night revellers. Like so many other hamlets, 'Candleford Green' was essentially 'law-abiding'.[32]

The relationship between crime and protest in the years before the establishment of a permanent trade union is a particularly difficult matter. Inevitably there is a danger of romanticizing men and gangs who were regarded by working men themselves as private adventurers, willing to exploit the poor and their grievances.[33] Certain offences, however, especially arson, sometimes reflected community anger, and there were others which were overwhelmingly crimes of protest. The sending of threatening letters falls into this category, and the early 1840s saw perhaps the last major outbreak of this form of intimidation. Where this attempt to enforce better conditions failed, labourers resorted, much more than we realize, to the killing and maiming of birds and animals (see pages 75–7).[34] In years of tension, such as 1837, 1842, and 1849, hundreds of pheasants were poisoned and cattle injured in East Anglia and the counties of the south-west. The periodic attacks on farm machinery formed another reminder of workmen's willingness to break the law in their fight for work and better wages. Between 1815 and the 1860s two generations of East Anglian farmers bought threshing machines, ploughs, and hoes only to see them destroyed by hammer and fire.[35]

Occasionally the frustration of labourers erupted in major explosions of unrest which covered a large area of the British countryside. Such outbursts occurred in the 1790s, 1816–19, 1822–3, and 1830–1, and their epicentre was usually East Anglia and the counties of the south-east. The events of 1830–1, the so-called 'Last Labourers' Revolt', have been well documented by Professors Hobsbawm and Rudé, though subsequent research suggests that the rising was even more widespread and complex than they described. Most counties south of the Scottish border had their share of threatening letters and incendiarism. At their meetings the labourers voiced complaints about many secondary issues from tithes and new machinery to the influx of Irish workers, and on these matters they found certain farmers unexpectedly sympathetic; but the heart of their message was 'more work and higher wages'. The fear which the Swing mobs engendered was reflected in the terrible judicial revenge taken by the authorities: 19 people executed, some 500 transported, and 644 imprisoned.[36]

A few years later another series of protests greeted the Poor Law Amendment Act and its implementation in East Anglia and various counties of the south and south-west. When the Rev. Maberley of Bourn in Cambridgeshire and a few other respectable leaders took the initiative in calling public meetings against the Act the labourers attended in good numbers, but generally violence was the response. Between 1834 and 1844 riots, arson, and attacks on the person and property of guardians were common occurrences in the affected counties. Sometimes labourers tore down half-built workhouses with their bare hands. The climaxes in this particular contest included the bloody 'Battle of Bossenden Wood' in Kent (1838), the attack on Carmarthen workhouse (1843), and the Great Bircham affair in Norfolk (1835), when 800 men confronted soldiers and policemen drafted in to enforce the new government policy.[37]

Between 1839 and 1844 the poor law question merged with more pressing problems of low farm prices, unemployment, and wage-cuts. The consequent discontent has been hardly studied by historians, except in two areas. In south-west Wales the accumulated anger of tenant-farmers and labourers exploded in the savage Rebecca riots. These riots, famous for the destruction of toll gates and the burning of farm property, were the occasion for a community rebellion.[38] In many other parts of the country, too, there were angry meetings of labourers, violent demonstrations, and a quite extraordinary wave of incendiarism. I discovered evidence of a minimum of 250 fires on the property of farmers, clergymen, and poor law guardians in Norfolk and Suffolk during the period October 1843–December 1844.[39] Villages in Bedfordshire and Cambridgeshire were literally put to the torch. In later years, notably 1849–52, 1862–4, and 1868–9, unrest was again common in the south and east and arson remained a popular form of intimidation; but of greater interest to historians was the slow growth of rural trade unionism.

All these protests were characterized by their localized nature. They were often well organized and supported by the village community, but links between districts were tenuous. The demonstrations and disturbances were also non-political in a formal sense. Political reformers had an influence on the Swing and Rebecca mobs, but generally the rioters were inspired by a sense of injustice and feelings of revenge.[40] The crime and protest of the first half of the nineteenth century were those of a depressed people, although there were interesting lines of development and shifts in consciousness. If by the 1860s some of the ferocity and vision of lost rights had gone, many labourers entered the trade union era with a greater sense of purpose and independence.

There are at least four important questions to be asked about crime and protest in this period. First, who committed the offences? The myth of the criminal outsider was strong, and had some basis in fact in villages close to large urban centres. The Swing and Rebecca riots were said to have been organized by 'suspicious strangers', and rural crime was attributed to vagrants, gipsies, and navvies. One recent analysis of criminal records, however, indicates that theft and violence in the countryside were usually committed by residents.[41] Some of these were members of criminal families and gangs, but the concept of a criminal class with its own sub-culture is hardly relevant to the rural scene. Many rural criminals, including thousands of poachers, were ordinary working men.[42] Arsonists, too, were often young farm labourers with no criminal past. Mobs could be a cross-section of the village population, with its more independent members to the fore. And, finally, there is overwhelming evidence that certain offenders operated with the support of most of the community; people protected wanted men, cheered outside courtrooms, and refused to act as special constables or fire-fighters.[43]

The second question is more complex. What did direct action achieve? We know, for instance, that jobs were saved by it, wage-cuts reversed, mechanization halted, and poor law allowances increased.[44] In some areas these successes added to the self-respect and confidence of workmen, but the reverse also seems to have been true. Villages decimated by the transportations and emigrations of the 1830s and 1840s, or stifled by the tight control of the gentry, sometimes developed that bleak fatalism, religious and otherwise, which George Sturt and others discovered many years later.[45] All protests, however, had one common result: they drew public attention to the plight of the labourer, and produced a variety of economic, educational, and social initiatives. In the aftermath of each major explosion, new charitable and recreational enterprises were begun, designed to bring classes closer together. Allotments were undoubtedly the most fruitful economic response, though migration and emigration schemes were popular in times such as the late 1840s and early 1850s.[46]

The third question is one which intrigued contemporaries – why did crime and rioting decline in the second half of the nineteenth century? It is a difficult question because this movement in the crime rates was apparently a phenomenon of the western world, and must have been linked to major economic developments, processes of social change, and new policing methods.[47] As we saw earlier, the last factor had a considerable impact on life in the countryside. So did the improved employment and wage situation in the mid-Victorian years and the greater ease of mobility consequent upon railways. Perhaps the most complex influences were changes in habits and attitudes. Joseph Arch and others claimed that people had become more law-abiding and less tolerant of those who got their living 'on the side'.[48] If this were so, it had long been an objective of the gentry. Allotments, enclosures, and poor law schemes were both economic and moral experiments, and we still know very little of the efforts made to denigrate and remove the independent elements in the village.[49] There is evidence, too, that in the 1840s and 1850s the rioter, the poacher, and the machine breaker were losing much of the crucial support that tenant farmers had once given them.[50] Even so, it may well be that changes in attitude and action by working people were the result not of external pressures but of internal ones.

This brings us to the final question of the relationship between direct action and peaceful methods of protest in the Victorian countryside. It is worth emphasizing that workers' anger took many forms, both before and after the critical years of the 1860s and 1870s. The village meetings, petitions, and union activities of Arch's early campaigns had their precursors in most of the southern and eastern counties a generation earlier. Between 1838 and 1846 political meetings and local unions were more common in the country than historians have hitherto realized. Similarly, in the Great Depression illegal acts of intimidation enjoyed a revival in the south. Yet the connections between criminal and peaceful forms of protest do not appear to have been strong, even during some of the Swing troubles. Although the poacher, the arsonist, and the union activist often had similar grievances and worked a close regional furrow, there were differences in support, organization, and method. The first union leaders were older men and had developed their values, priorities, and organizational skills in the militant Nonconformist chapels which had spread like a rash over the countryside during their lifetime. The climate of political and social change and the labourers' improved bargaining position gave these men the advantage, and the underground terrorism of the earlier years gradually faded away.

Notes

1 Dunbabin, 1974, 27.
2 Plint, 1851. Note the biased account of country life in publications like the *League*, and in the evidence of Chadwick and Bright in BPP 1839 XIX; 1846 IX.
3 *Journal of Royal Statistical Society*, XIX, i.
4 For this paragraph, see *Morning Chronicle*, 29 December 1849, Jones and Bainbridge, 1975, and especially the evidence in BPP 1839 XIX, and 1852–3 XXXVI.
5 BPP 1839 XIX; 1852–3, XXXVI. See also Horn, 1976b, 219–21.
6 Glyde, 1856a, 133; Jones and Bainbridge, 1975.
7 Worsley, 1849, ch. 2. Compare Glyde, 1856a, 147.
8 Flora Thompson, 1973, 291.
9 Holdenby, 1913, 26–7.
10 Hobsbawm and Rudé, 1969, 38–55, 72–93; Amos, 1971, 41–5, 165; *Social History*, I, i, 27–32; *Morning Chronicle*, 8 and 22 December 1849.
11 *Journal of Social History*, VII; E. P. Thompson, 1975; Jones, 1973; Hay *et al.*, 1975.
12 For example, Reaney, 1970; *Llafur*, I, iii, 7.
13 Henslow, 1844, 18; Dunbabin, 1974, 46; Samuel, 1975b, 53–61.
14 Some conception of the importance of charity rights and land can be gained from the reminiscences of Ashby, 1961, and Haggard, 1935.
15 For popular opposition to changes in the administration of poor relief prior to 1834, see Amos, 1971, 82–3; Digby, 1972, 168–80; Peacock, 1965, 31–42; Hobsbawm and Rudé, 1969, 69.
16 It is difficult, as Thomas Campbell Foster found, to establish a precise connection between anger over fear of the workhouse and the readiness to commit the crimes, but the evidence of prison chaplains and the prisoners

themselves leaves little room for doubt. See, for instance, the evidence of F. Gowing in BPP 1846 IX pt I, 629, and prison reports for Suffolk and Norfolk in BPP 1844 XXIX, and 1846 XXI. See also Glyde, 1856a, 185–7.

17 For remarks about the decline of traditional forms of amusement, the boredom of young workmen, and their capacity for drink and crime see Henslow, 1844, 25–6; Kay-Shuttleworth, 1971, I, 604–5, 612–13; Howkins, 1973.

18 See Amos, 1971, 167–70; *Social History*, I, i, 14; Hobsbawm and Rudé, 1969, 59, 81–2.

19 See Wrigley, 1972, 136–96.

20 The following paragraphs are based on a study of the criminal statistics in BPP 1835–92.

21 See, for instance, BPP 1839 XIX 38–42.

22 *Morning Chronicle*, 19 August 1844; BPP 1849 XLIV 448–50; 1862 XLV 222–8. The Staffordshire figure is based on a study of the *Staffordshire Advertizer* for the period. Such violence occurred on a somewhat lesser scale at a later date. See Horn, 1976b, 233, and the story of assaults on, and murders of, water bailiffs in BPP 1872 X 45, 57–8, 62–3, and in the *Carlisle Journal*, 17 January 1862, 21 January, and 22 February 1870.

23 See BPP 1839 XIX, 1852–3 XXXVI; Dunbabin, 1974, 27–61; Horn, 1976b, 219–38.

24 BPP 1846 IX pt I, 784; 1872 X, app. 4. Between 1845 and 1871, two fairly average years, the number of people in England and Wales committed under the game laws doubled to some 10,000 (excluding 929 under the new Poaching Prevention Act).

25 The later nineteenth century saw some final and brutal confrontations between poaching gangs, keepers, and the police: Horn, 1976b, 233; *Llafur*, II, i. For new evidence on poaching and assaults in a previous era, see Hay *et al.*, 1975, 189–253; Cockburn, 1977, 210–28.

26 See BPP 1839 XIX 38, 131, 134. The best starting-point for the Welsh conflict is the extensive report in BPP 1896 XXXIV.

27 Dunbabin, 1974, 30–6, 52–3, 56–69, 62–70; Caird, 1968, 420, 467–8; Olney, 1975, 26; *Morning Chronicle*, letters of December 1849 – January 1850.

28 *Welsh History Review*, VIII, iii, 335.

29 As far as I know, little research has been done on this form of protest. John Glyde said that 807 people were moved from seven workhouses to Ipswich gaol between 1844 and 1852; Glyde, 1856a, 187.

30 *Welsh History Review*, VIII, iii. See the many references to vagrancy in BPP 1852–3 XXXVI. Ribton-Turner, 1887, is still useful.

31 The battle against alcohol was particularly interesting in Wales and the south-west, but one wonders just how much could have been drunk: Glyde, 1856a, 359; Flora Thompson, 1973, 65. For the verdict on the sobriety or otherwise of the labourer at the end of the century see BPP 1893–4 XXXV.

32 Flora Thompson, 1973, 479–84; Horn, 1976b, 237–8.

33 A good deal was made of the anger of working people at certain criminal activity, and of their willingness to use the new police and the law for their protection. See, for instance, BPP 1852–3 XXXVI 21, 68, 127. The former was certainly true, but one should not underestimate the suspicion both of the legitimacy of the property law and of the new police in the countryside. Compare Philips, 1977, 285.

34 The only published account of this prior to this volume is in Dunbabin,

1974, 27–61. Hobsbawm and Rudé, 1969, 80, underestimated the popularity of this crime.

35 The men attacked machinery for a variety of reasons. See Samuel, 1975b, 61–6; Amos, 1971, 21–4; Peacock, 1965, 70; and pp. 46–7 in this volume.
36 Hobsbawm and Rudé, 1969; Amos, 1971; *International Review of Social History*, XIX.
37 Digby, 1972, 170–5; Amos, 1971, 82–3, 91–2, 172–3, ch. VIII; Dunbabin, 1974, 36–9; Springall, 1936, 27–31. Some of the East Anglian story can be followed in the *Norwich Mercury*, 1834–6, and PRO: HO 52/26, 73/6–7.
38 David Williams, 1955.
39 *Social History*, I, i.
40 Amos, 1971, 118; Hobsbawm and Rudé, 1969, 65–6, 89–90.
41 Jones and Bainbridge, 1975, 245–346; *Welsh History Review*, VIII, iii, 324–8.
42 See BPP 1845 XXIV 174, 186, and 1846 IX pt I, 630, pt II, 313. On the other hand, there were gangs in the countryside around Stoke-on-Trent, Nottingham, Chester, and Norwich, which seem to have existed almost exclusively by well-organized poaching and stealing. See, for instance, BPP 1839 XIX 113.
43 *Social History*, I, i, 16–17; Dunbabin, 1974, 34–5, 52–3; Amos, 1971, 91, 108–12, 161. Sometimes workmen seemed keen to help the authorities, but the reasons for this varied: Amos, 1971, 65, 91.
44 E. P. Thompson, 1974, 228; Hobsbawm and Rudé, 1969, 281.
45 Hobsbawm and Rudé, 1969, 288–91.
46 *Social History*, I, i, 35–6. The subject of allotments deserves a major study; their introduction was said to have brought about a great reduction in crime: *Morning Chronicle*, 26 December 1849.
47 Zehr, 1976; Gurr, Grabovsky, and Hula, 1977.
48 For this, see BPP 1872 X: evidence of Donne and Arch; Ashby, 1961, 3–4.
49 *Longman's Magazine*, July 1883. The question of social control in the village is a difficult subject. Social activities and behaviour were transformed in places, but observers suspected that the mind and solidarity of villagers remained untouched. Howkins, 1973, 44; BPP 1893–4 XXXV pt I, 13, pt II, 19, and many other entries. On the other hand, there had always been subtle differences within villages.
50 David Williams, 1955, 243; Reaney, 1970, 68. Where, as in Wales and Hertfordshire, poaching activities threatened to turn into a wider attack on property rights, the limitations of non-working-class help were obvious: BPP 1846 IX: evidence of Robertson and Pearce. Significantly, many landowners allowed tenant-farmers to kill a greater share of the ground game in mid-Victorian years.

References

Abbiateci, André, 1978, 'Arsonists in eighteenth century France: an essay in the typology of crime', in R. Forster, and O. Ranum (eds), *Deviants and the Abandoned in French Society: Selection from the 'Annales'*, IV, Johns Hopkins University Press, Baltimore.

Amos, S. W., 1971, 'Social discontent and agrarian disturbances in Essex 1795–1850', unpublished MA thesis, University of Durham, Durham.

Andrews, C. B. (ed.), 1954, *The Torrington Diaries*, Eyre & Spottiswoode, London.

Arch, Joseph, 1898, *Joseph Arch: The Story of his Life, Told by Himself*, Hutchinson, London.

Arch, Joseph, (1898) 1986, *From Ploughtail to Parliament: An Autobiography*, Cresset Library, London.

Archer, John E., 1982a, 'The Wells-Charlesworth debate: a personal comment on arson in Norfolk and Suffolk', *Journal of Peasant Studies*, IX, 4.

—— 1982b, 'Rural protest in Norfolk and Suffolk 1830–1870', unpublished Ph.D. thesis, University of East Anglia, Norwich.

—— 1982c, 'Rural protest in Norfolk and Suffolk 1830–1870', in Andrew Charlesworth (ed.), *Rural Social Change and Conflicts since 1500*, Coral, Hull.

—— 1985, ' "A fiendish outrage"? A study of animal maiming in East Anglia 1830–1870', *Agricultural History Review*, XXXIII, 2.

Arnold, R., 1974, 'The "Revolt of the field" in Kent 1872–92', *Past and Present*, LXIV.

Ashby, J. and King, B., 1893, 'Statistics of some Midland villages', *Economic Journal*, III.

Ashby, M. K., 1961, *Joseph Ashby of Tysoe 1857–1919*, Cambridge University Press, Cambridge.

—— 1974, *The Changing English Village 1066–1914*, Roundwood Press, Kineton, Warwickshire.

Barnes, T. G., 1959, *Somerset Assize Orders 1629–1640*, Somerset Record Society, LXV, Frome.

Bawn, K. P., 1984, 'Social protest, popular disturbances and public order in Dorset, 1790–1838', unpublished Ph.D. thesis, University of Reading, Reading.

Beattie, J. M., 1974, 'The pattern of crime in England 1660–1800', *Past and Present*, LXII.

——1975, 'The criminality of women in eighteenth-century England', *Journal of Social History*, VIII.

——1986, *Crime and the Courts in England 1660–1800*, Clarendon Press, Oxford.

Beier, A. J., 1974, 'Vagrants and the social order in Elizabethan England', *Past and Present*, LXIV.

Beresford, J., 1967, *Woodforde: The Diary of a Country Parson, 1758–1802*, Oxford University Press, Oxford.

Bohstedt, J., 1983, *Riots and Community Politics in England and Wales*, Harvard University Press, Cambridge, Mass.

Bowley, A. L., 1898, 'The statistics of wages in the United Kingdom during the last hundred years, part one', *Journal of the Royal Statistical Society*, LXI, December.

Bridenbaugh, Carl, 1968, *Vexed and Troubled Englishmen*, Oxford University Press, Oxford.

BPP (British Parliamentary Papers), 1839 XIX RC Constabulary Force.

——1844 XXIX Inspectors' reports on prisons.

——1845 XXIV Inspectors' reports on prisons.

——1846 IX SC Game Laws.

——1846 XXI Inspectors' reports on prisons.

——1849 XLIV Returns of persons killed and injured in poaching affrays.

——1852–3 XXXVI parts I and II 1851 census. Population tables, II, vols I and II.

——1861 XXI RC State of popular education in England (Newcastle Commission).

——1862 XLV Memorial from chief constables and return of murderous assaults on gamekeepers in 1859.

——1872 X SC Game Laws.

——1872 XXVI RC Friendly Societies, minutes of evidence.

——1873 XIII SC Game Laws.

——1889 LIX Return of School Boards and attendance committees, 1889.

——1893–4 XXXV RC Labour: the agricultural labourer (England).

——1896 XXXIV RC Land in Wales and Monmouthshire, Report

Burnett, John, 1978, *A Social History of Housing, 1815–1970*, David & Charles, Newton Abbot.

Bushaway, Bob, 1982, *By Rite: Custom, Ceremony and Community in England 1700–1880*, Junction Books, London.

Caird, James, (1852) 1968, *English Agriculture in 1850–51*, new edn, Frank Cass, London.

Carson, Edward, 1972, *The Ancient and Rightful Customs*, Faber, London.

Carter, Clive, 1970, *Cornish Shipwrecks, II*, David & Charles, Newton Abbot.

Carter, Michael J., 1980, *Peasants and Poachers*, Boydell Press, Woodbridge, Suffolk.

Charlesworth, Andrew, 1978, *Social Protest in a Rural Society: The Spatial Diffusion of the Captain Swing Disturbances of 1830–31*, Historical Geography Research Series, No. 1, Geo Books, Norwich.

——1980, 'The development of the English rural proletariat and social protest, 1700–1850: a comment', *Journal of Peasant Studies*, VIII, 1.

——1983, *An Atlas of Rural Protest in Britain, 1548–1900*, Croom Helm, Beckenham.

Chenevix-Trench, Charles P., 1967, *The Poacher and the Squire: A History of Poaching and Game Preservation in England*, Longman, Harlow.

Clark, Peter, 1978, 'The alehouse and alternative society', in Donald Pennington and Keith Thomas (eds), *Puritans and Revolutions*, Oxford University Press, Oxford.

Cobbett, William, (1830) 1912, *Rural Rides*, Everyman edn, Dent, London.

——1967, *Rural Rides*, ed. G. Woodcock, Penguin, Harmondsworth.

Cockburn, J. S., 1965, 'The North Riding justices 1690–1750', *Yorkshire Archaeological Journal*, XLI.

——1976, *Western Circuit Assize Orders 1629–1648*, Royal Historical Society, Camden, 4th Series.

Cockburn, J. S. (ed.), 1977, *Crime in England 1550–1800*, Methuen, London.

Coleman, H., 1844, 'The agricultural labourers of England', *The Labourer's Friend*, August.

Coxe, A. D. Hippesley, 1984, *Smuggling in the West Country 1700–1850*, Tabb House, Padstow, Cornwall.

Curtis, T. C., 1977, 'Quarter sessions appearances and their background: a seventeenth-century regional study', in J. S. Cockburn (ed.), *Crime in England 1550–1800*, Methuen, London.

de Montmorency, J. E. G., 1902, 'State protection of animals at home and abroad', *Law Quarterly Review*, XVIII.

Digby, A., 1972, 'The operation of the poor law in the social and economic life of nineteenth-century Norfolk', unpublished Ph.D. thesis, University of East Anglia, Norwich.

——1978, *Pauper Palaces*, Routledge & Kegan Paul, London.

Dodd, J. P., 1965, 'South Lancashire in transition: a study of the crop returns for 1795–1801', *Transactions of the Historical Society of Lancashire and Cheshire*, CXVII.

Dunbabin, J. P. D., 1974, *Rural Discontent in Nineteenth-Century Britain*, Faber & Faber, London.

Eden, Sir F. M., 1966, *The State of the Poor*, new edn, Frank Cass, London.

Emmison, F. G., 1970, *Elizabethan Life, I: Disorder*, Essex Record Office, Chelmsford.

Engels, F., 1950, *The Condition of the Working Class in England in 1844*, new edn, Blackwell, Oxford.

Evans, George Ewart, 1960, *The Horse in the Furrow*, Faber, London.

——1970, *Where Beards Wag All: The Relevance of the Oral Tradition*, Faber, London.

Forster, G. C. F., 1973, *The East Riding Justices of the Peace in the Seventeenth Century*, East Yorkshire Local History Series, XXX, East Yorkshire Local History Society, York.

——1975, 'The North Riding justices and their sessions 1603–1625', *Northern History*, X.

Fox, N. E., 1978, 'The spread of the threshing machine in central southern England', *Agricultural History Review*, XXVI, 1.

Fraser's Magazine, 1844, 'Incendiarism, its causes and cure'.

Girouard, Mark, 1978, *Life in the English Country House: A Social and Architectural History*, Yale University Press, New Haven, Conn.

Glyde, J., 1856a, 'Localities of crime in Suffolk', *Journal of the Royal Statistical Society of London*, XIX, 1.

——1856b, *Suffolk in the Nineteenth Century*, J. M. Burton, London.

——1894, 'The autobiography of a Suffolk farm labourer', *Suffolk Mercury*, Ipswich.

Gosden, P. H. J. H., 1961, *The Friendly Societies in England 1815–1875*, Manchester University Press, Manchester.

Green, F. E., 1913, *The Tyranny of the Countryside*, T. Fisher Unwin, London.

——1920, *A History of the English Agricultural Labourer, 1870–1920*, P. S. King, London.

Gurden, Helen, 1976, 'Primitive methodism and agricultural trade unionism in Warwickshire, 1872–75', *Bulletin of the Society for the Study of Labour History*, XXXIII.

Gurr, T. R., Grabovsky, P. N., and Hula, R. C., 1977, *The Politics of Crime and Conflict*, Sage Publishing, Beverly Hills, Calif.

Guttridge, Roger, 1987, *Dorset Smugglers*, Dorset Publishing Company, Milborne Port, Dorset.

Hammond, J. L. and Hammond, B., 1920, *The Village Labourer 1760–1832*, Longman, Harlow.

——(1920) 1978, *The Village Labourer 1760–1832*, Longman, Harlow.

Harber, J., 1975, 'Incendiarism in Suffolk, 1840–45', unpublished MA thesis, University of Essex, Colchester.

Hawker, James, 1978, *A Victorian Poacher: James Hawker's Journal*, Oxford University Press, Oxford.

Hay, D., 1982, 'War, dearth and theft in the eighteenth century: the record of the English courts', *Past and Present*, XCV.

Hay, D., Linebaugh, P., Rule, J. G., Thompson, E. P., and Winslow, C. (eds), 1975, *Albion's Fatal Tree: Crime and Society in Eighteenth-Century England*, Allen Lane, London.

Heath, R., (1893) 1978, *The English Peasant*, new edn, E. P. Publishing, Wakefield.

Henslow, J. S., 1844, *Suggestions towards and Enquiry into the Present Condition of the Labouring Population of Suffolk*, Hadleigh, Suffolk.

Herrup, Cynthia B., 1985, 'Law and morality in seventeenth-century England', *Past and Present*, CVI.

Hey, D. G., 1974, *An English Rural Community, Myddle*, Leicester University Press, Leicester.

Hine, Richard, 1928, 'Friendly Societies and their emblems', *Proceedings of the Dorset Natural History and Antiquarian Field Club*, XLIX.

Hobsbawm, E. J. and Rudé, G., 1969, *Captain Swing*, Lawrence & Wishart, London.

——(1969) 1973, *Captain Swing*, Penguin, Harmondsworth.

Hodder, E., 1887, *The Life and Work of the Seventh Earl of Shaftesbury*, Cassell, London.

Holdenby, C., 1913, *Folk of the Furrow*, Smith Elder, London.

Holderness, B. A., 1972, ' "Open and close" parishes in England in the eighteenth and nineteenth centuries', *Agricultural History Review*, XX, 2.

Hopkins, H., 1985, *The Long Affray: The Poaching Wars in Britain*, Secker & Warburg, London.

Horn, Pamela, 1971, *Joseph Arch (1826–1919), The Farm Workers' Leader*, Roundwood Press, Kineton, Warwicks.

——1972, 'Agricultural trade unionism and emigration, 1872–1881', *Historical Journal*, XV, 1.

——1973, 'The Gawcott revolt of 1867', *Records of Buckinghamshire*, XIX, 3.
——1974a, *Agricultural Trade Unionism in Oxfordshire 1972–81*, Oxfordshire Record Society, XLVIII, Oxford.
——1974b, 'Landowners and the agricultural trade union movement of the 1870s', *Local Historian*, II, 3.
——1976a, 'Agricultural unionism and emigration', *Historical Journal*, XVII.
——1976b, *Labouring Life in the Victorian Countryside*, Gill & Macmillan, Dublin.
——1980, *The Rural World, 1780–1850*, Hutchinson, London.
Howkins, Alun, 1973, *Whitsun in Nineteenth Century Oxfordshire*, History Workshop Pamphlet No. 8, Ruskin College, Oxford.
——1979, 'Economic crime and class law: poaching and the game laws, 1840–80', in S. B. Burman and B. E. Harrell-Bond (eds), *Imposition of the Law*, Academic Press, London.
Hudson, W. H., (1910) 1911, *A Shepherd's Life*, 3rd edn, Methuen, London.
Hurt, J., 1968, 'Landowners, farmers and clergy in the financing of rural education before 1870', *Journal of Education Administration and History*, I, 1.
——1971, *Education in Evolution*, Paladin, London.

Ingram, M. J., 1977, 'Communities and courts: law and disorder in early seventeenth-century Wiltshire', in J. S. Cockburn (ed.), *Crime in England 1550–1800*, Methuen, London.
Innes, Joanna and Styles, John, 1986, 'The crime wave: recent writing on crime and criminal justice in eighteenth-century England', *Journal of British Studies*, XXV.
Itzkowitz, D. C., 1977, *Peculiar Privilege: A Social History of English Foxhunting 1753–1885*, Harvester Press, Hassocks.

Jackson, C. H. Ward, 1986, *Ships and Shipbuilders of a West Country Seaport: Fowey 1786–1939*, Twelveheads Press, Truro, Cornwall.
Jamieson, Alan G., 1986, *A People of the Sea: The Maritime History of the Channel Islands*, Methuen, London.
Jenkin, A. K. Hamilton, 1932, *Cornish Seafarers*, Dent, London.
Johnson, Derek, 1981, *Victorian Shooting Days: East Anglia, 1810–1910*, Boydell Press, Woodbridge, Suffolk.
Jones, D. J. V., 1973, *Before Rebecca: Popular Protests in Wales, 1793–1835*, Allen Lane, London.
——1976a, 'Thomas Campbell Foster and the rural labourer: incendiarism in East Anglia in the 1840s', *Social History*, I.
——1976b, 'The second Rebecca riots', *Llafur*, II, 1.
——1977, 'The criminal vagrant in mid-nineteenth century Wales', *Welsh Historical Review*, VIII, 3.
——1979, 'The poacher: a study in Victorian crime and protest', *Historical Journal*, XXII.
——1982, *Crime, Protest, Community and Police in Nineteenth Century Britain*, Routledge & Kegan Paul, London.
Jones, D. J. V. and Bainbridge, A., 1975, *Crime in Nineteenth-Century Wales*, Social Science Research Council Report, University College, Swansea.
Journal of the Statistical Society of London, 1845, 'Incendiarism', VIII.

Kay-Shuttleworth, J. P., 1971, *The Social Condition and Education of the People, I*, Irish University Press, Shannon.

King, P. J. R., 1984, 'Decision makers and decision making in the English criminal law 1750–1800', *Historical Journal*, XXVII.

King, Walter J., 1980, 'Leet jurors and the search for law and order in seventeenth-century England', *Social History*, XIII.

Kirby, Chester, 1932, 'The attack on the game laws in the forties', *Journal of Modern History*, IV.

Kussmaul, Ann, 1981, *Servants in Husbandry in Early Modern England*, Cambridge University Press, Cambridge.

Lowerson, J., 1982, 'The aftermath of Swing: anti-poor law movements and rural trade unions in the south-east of England', in Andrew Charlesworth (ed.), *Rural Social Change and Conflicts since 1500*, Coral, Hull.

Macdonald, Stuart, 1975, 'The progress of the early threshing machine', *Agricultural History Review*, XXIII, 1.

——1978, 'Further progress with the early threshing machine', *Agricultural History Review*, XXVI, 1.

Macfarlane, Alan, 1981, *The Justice and the Mare's Ale*, Blackwell, Oxford.

Marchant, R. A., 1969, *The Church under the Law: Diocese of York 1560–1640*, Cambridge University Press, Cambridge.

Mingay, G. E., 1961–2, 'The size of farms in the eighteenth century', *Economic History Review*, 2nd ser., XIV.

Morley, Geoffrey, 1983, *Smuggling in Hampshire and Dorset 1700–1850*, Countryside Books, Newbury, Berks.

Morrill, J. S., 1976, *The Cheshire Grand Jury, 1625–1659*, Leicester University Press, Leicester.

Munsche, P. B., 1981a, *Gentlemen and Poachers*, Cambridge University Press, Cambridge.

——1981b, 'The gamekeeper and English rural society, 1661–1830', *Journal of British Studies*, XX.

Muskett, P., 1986, 'Deal smugglers in the eighteenth century', *Southern History*, VIII.

Olney, R. J. (ed.), 1975, *Labouring Life on the Lincolnshire Wolds: A Study of Binbrook in the Mid-Nineteenth Century*, Society for Lincolnshire History and Archaeology, Sleaford.

Orwin, C. S. and Whetham, E. H., 1964, *History of British Agriculture, 1846–1914*, Longman, Harlow.

Peacock, A. J., 1962, 'Land reform, 1880–1914', unpublished MA thesis, University of Southampton, Southampton.

——1965, *Bread or Blood*, Gollancz, London.

——1974, 'Village radicalism in East Anglia, 1800–1850, in J. P. D. Dunbabin (ed.), *Rural Discontent in Nineteenth Century Britain*, Faber, London.

Pellew, G., 1847, *Life and Correspondence of First Viscount Sidmouth*, Murray, London.

Pevsner, Nikolaus, 1972, *The Buildings of England: Yorkshire: York and the East Riding*, Penguin, Harmondsworth.

Philips, D., 1977, *Crime and Authority in Victorian England*, Croom Helm, Beckenham.

Plint, T., 1851, *Crime in England, Its Relation, Character and Extent as Developed from 1801 to 1848*, C. Gilpin, London.

Porter, J. H., 1982, 'Poaching and social conflict in late Victorian Devon', in Andrew Charlesworth (ed.), *Rural Social Change and Conflicts since 1500*, Coral, Hull.
——1989, 'The development of rural society', in G. E. Mingay (ed.), *The Agrarian History of England and Wales, VI 1750–1850*, Cambridge University Press, Cambridge.

Radzinowicz, Sir Leon, 1948, *A History of English Criminal Law and its Administration, I*, Stevens & Sons, London.
Rattenbury, John, 1837, *Memoirs of a Smuggler*, Harvey, Sidmouth, Devon.
Reaney, B., 1970, *The Class Struggle in Nineteenth-Century Oxfordshire*, History Workshop Pamphlet No. 3, Ruskin College, Oxford.
Ribton-Turner, C. J., 1887, *A History of Vagrants and Vagrancy*, Chapman and Hall, London.
Rider Haggard, L. (ed.), (1935) 1974, *I Walked by Night*, Boydell Press, Ipswich.
Rudé, George, 1964, *The Crowd in History*, Wiley, New York.
——1978, *Protest and Punishment*, Oxford University Press, Oxford.
Rule, John, 1975, 'Wrecking and coastal plunder', in D. Hay, *et al.* (eds), *Albion's Fatal Tree*, Allen Lane, London.
——1979, 'Social crime in the rural south in the eighteenth and early nineteenth centuries', *Southern History*, I.
——1982, *Outside the Law: Studies in Crime and Order 1650–1850*, University of Exeter, Exeter.
——1986, *The Labouring Classes in Early Industrial England, 1750–1850*, Longman, Harlow.
Russell, Rex C., n.d. (c. 1956), *The 'revolt of the field' in Lincolnshire*, National Union of Agricultural Workers, Lincolnshire County Committee, Lincoln.
——1975, *Friendly Societies in the Caistor, Binbrook and Brigg Area in the Nineteenth Century*, Workers' Educational Association, Nettleton Branch, Lincs.

Sage, Josiah, 1951, *Memoirs of Josiah Sage*, Lawrence & Wishart, London.
Samuel, Raphael, 1975a, 'Quarry roughs: life and labour in Headington Quarry, 1860–1920. An essay in oral history', in Raphael Samuel (ed.), *Village Life and Labour*, Routledge & Kegan Paul, London.
——1975b, *Village Life and Labour*, Routledge & Kegan Paul, London.
Scotland, Nigel A. D., 1977, 'Methodism and the "Revolt of the Field" in East Anglia, 1872–96', *Proceedings of the Wesley Historical Society* XLI, 1.
Selley, Ernest, 1919, *Village Trade Unions in Two Centuries*, Allen & Unwin, London.
Sharpe, J. A., 1977, 'Crime and delinquency in an Essex parish 1600–1640', in J. S. Cockburn (ed.), *Crime in England 1550–1800*, Methuen, London.
——1980a, *Defamation and Sexual Slander in Early Modern England: The Church Courts at York*, Borthwick Papers, LVIII, York.
——1980b, 'Enforcing the law in the seventeenth-century English village', in V. A. C. Gatrell, Bruce Lenman, and Geoffrey Parker (eds), *Crime and the Law: The Social History of Crime in Western Europe since 1500*, Europa, London.
——1983, *Crime in Seventeenth-Century England: A County Study*, Cambridge University Press, Cambridge.
——1984, *Crime in Early Modern England 1550–1750*, Longman, London.
Shelton, W. J., 1973, *English Hunger and Industrial Disorders*, Macmillan, London.

Slack, P. A., 1974, 'Vagrants and vagrancy in England, 1598–1664', *Economic History Review*, 2nd ser., XXVII, 3.

Smith, C., 1766, *Three Tracts on the Corn Trade and Corn Laws*, 2nd edn.

Spater, George, 1982, *William Cobbett: The Poor Man's Friend*, Cambridge University Press, Cambridge.

Springall, L. Marion, 1936, *Labouring Life in Norfolk Villages, 1834–1914*, Allen & Unwin, London.

Stevenson, J., 1974, 'Food riots in England, 1792–1818', in J. Stevenson and R. Quinault (eds), *Popular Protest and Public Order*, Allen & Unwin, London.

——1979, *Popular Disturbances in England, 1700–1870*, Longman, Harlow.

Taine, Hyppolyte, 1957, *Notes on England*, trans. Edward Hyams, Thames & Hudson, London.

Thomas, Stanley, 1959, *The 'nightingale' scandal*, Gazette Printing, Bideford, Devon.

Thompson, E. P., 1965, *The Making of the English Working Class*, Gollancz, London.

——1971, 'The moral economy of the English crowd in the eighteenth century', *Past and Present*, L.

——1974, 'Patrician society, plebeian culture', *Journal of Social History*, VII, 4.

——1975, *Whigs and Hunters: The Origin of the Black Act*, Allen Lane, London.

Thompson, Flora, (1939) 1973, *Lark Rise to Candleford*, new edn, Penguin, Harmondsworth.

Tilley, C., 1969, 'Collective violence in European perspective', in H. D. Graham and T. R. Gurr (eds), *The History of Violence in America*, Praeger, London.

Victoria County History: Essex VI, 1973, ed. W. R. Powell, Oxford University Press, Oxford.

Victoria County History: Gloucestershire XI, 1976, ed. N. M. Herbert, Oxford University Press, Oxford.

Victoria County History: Lincolnshire I, 1906, ed. W. Page, Archibald Constable, London.

Victoria County History: Middlesex V, 1976, ed. T. F. T. Baker, Oxford University Press, Oxford.

Victoria County History: Oxfordshire VIII, 1964, ed. Mary D. Lobel and Alan Crossley, Oxford University Press, Oxford.

Victoria County History: Oxfordshire IX, 1969, ed. Mary D. Lobel and Alan Crossley, Oxford University Press, Oxford.

Victoria County History: Oxfordshire X, 1972, ed. Alan Crossley, Oxford University Press, Oxford.

Victoria County History: Wiltshire X, 1975, ed. E. Crittall, Oxford University Press, Oxford.

Walter, J. and Wrightson, K., 1976, 'Dearth and the social order in early modern England', *Past and Present*, LXXI.

Wells, R. A. E., 1979, 'The development of the English rural proletariat and social protest, 1700–1800', *Journal of Peasant Studies*, VI, 2.

——1981, 'Social conflict and protest in the English countryside in the early nineteenth century: a rejoinder', *Journal of Peasant Studies*, VIII, 4.

——1984, 'Sheep rustling in Yorkshire in the age of the industrial and agrarian revolutions', *Northern History*, XX.

——1985, 'Rural rebels in southern England in the 1830s', in Clive Emsley and

James Walvin (eds), *Artisans, Peasants and Proletarians, 1760–1860*, Croom Helm, Beckenham.

Whetham, E. H., 1978, *The Agrarian History of England and Wales: VIII 1914–39*, Cambridge University Press, Cambridge.

Williams, David, 1955, *The Rebecca Riots*, University of Wales Press, Cardiff.

Williams, G. A., 1968, *Artisans and Sans-Culottes*, Arnold, London.

Winslow, Cal, 1975, 'Sussex smugglers', in D. Hay, *et al.* (eds), *Albion's Fatal Tree*, Allen Lane, London.

Wordie, J. R., 1974, 'Social change on the Leveson-Gower estates, 1714–1832', *Economic History Review*, 2nd ser., XXVII, 4.

Worsley, H., 1849, *Juvenile Depravity*, C. Galpin, London.

Wrightson, Keith, 1980, 'Two concepts of order: Justices, constables and jurymen in seventeenth-century England', in John Brewer and John Styles (eds), *An Ungovernable People*, Hutchinson, London.

——1981, 'Alehouses, order and reformation in rural England 1590–1660', in Eileen Yeo and Stephen Yeo (eds), *Popular Culture and Class Conflict 1590–1914*, Harvester Press, Brighton.

Wrightson, Keith and Levine, David, 1979, *Poverty and Piety in an English Village, Terling 1525–1700*, Academic Press, New York.

Wrigley, E. A. (ed.), 1972, *Nineteenth Century Society*, Cambridge University Press, Cambridge.

Young, A. (ed.), 1796, *Annals of Agriculture and Other Useful Arts*, XXV.

Zehr, H., 1976, *Crime and the Development of Modern Society*, Croom Helm, Beckenham.

Index

alehouses, 12–13; *see also* beerhouses

animal maiming, 50, 65, 75–7, 119; causes of, 75, 77; factors in, 75–6; scale of, 76

Arch, Joseph, 59, 62, 80, 83, 103–7, 121

arson, 6–7, 42–3, 44, 47–8, 49, 65–75, 112, 119; and literacy, 67; and other crimes, 71, 73; and unemployment, 68, 72, 75; and wages, 67, 71; as form of protest, 65–6, 118; attitudes to, 70–1, 74; background to, 66–9; factors in, 71–3; geographical pattern of, 69; punishment of, 72–3; scale of, 69–70, 117–18, 120

arsonists, character of, 67, 70, 72–4, 121

assault, 10–12, 14, 117, 118, 120

beerhouses, 116

Benett, Sir John, 45

Berkshire Agricultural Labourers' Union, 107

Black Act, 1723, 53, 65, 66

bread, consumption of, 24–5

Byng, John, 6

Caird, James, 37

charities, village, 115

clergy, 5, 44; and agricultural labourers' unions, 108–9; and education, 92; and tithes, 5, 41, 43, 44; benefit of, 18

close parishes, 95–7

Cobbett, William, 24, 36, 39, 40, 42–3, 49, 53, 68

crime, and food prices, 4, 14–15; and poachers, 62–3; and poverty, 17;

and punishment, 18–19; and war, 15; incidence of, 14–15, 112–15, 116, 121; prosecutions for, 113

defamation, 11, 17

Denbigh, Earl of, 104

drunkenness, 11–12, 118

Eastern Counties Labour Federation, 107

education, 89–93; and arson, 67; and clergy, 92; and landowners, 89–93

enclosure, 6, 46, 115

English Land Restoration League, 107, 108

farm servants, 1, 3, 40

farmers, and hunting, 87; and law enforcement, 19; and poachers, 121

farms, large-scale, 2–3, 40–1; size of, 2

food riots, 5, 23–34; and farm labourers, 33–4; and prices, 23–4, 26, 28–33; geographical pattern of, 33; of 1766–7, 26–7; of 1782–93, 27–8; of 1795–6, 28–9; of 1800–1, 30; of 1810–13, 31; of 1816–18, 31–2

Foster, Thomas Campbell, 67, 68, 74, 111

friendly societies, 99–101

game, preservation of, 82–9; geographical pattern of, 84–5; trade in game, 55, 60

Game Laws, 5–6, 40, 52–6, 62, 83

gamekeepers, 54–6, 62–3, 82–6, 88–9; casualties among, 63, 117; numbers of, 82, 84–6, 88–9

gleaning customs, 115